対訳
日本小史

JAPAN: A SHORT HISTORY

西海コエン *Nishiumi Coen*

IBCパブリッシング

装　　幀：斉藤啓（ブッダプロダクションズ）
編集協力：久松紀子

photo credit

© Katsuhiko Mizuno, p.31（熊野）

© National Land Image Information (Color Aerial Photographs), Ministry of Land, Infrastructure,
　Transport and Tourism, cover, p.18（仁徳天皇陵）

(via Wikimedia Commons)

Chris 73, cover, p.21（飛鳥大仏）[CC BY-SA 3.0]

Cquest, p.45（龍安寺）[CC BY-SA 2.5]

David Moore, p.51（楠木正成像）[CC BY-SA 2.5]

Elmo rainy day, p.8（弥生式土器）[CC BY-SA 3.0]

Galopin, cover, p.59（永楽通宝）

I, Sailko, p.8（縄文式土器）[GFDL or CC BY-SA 3.0]

Kakidai, p.11（勾玉）[CC BY-SA 3.0]

PHGCOM, p.10（銅鐸）[GFDL, CC-BY-SA-3.0 or CC BY-SA 2.5-2.0-1.0]

Wiiii, cover, p.27（東大寺金堂）, p.44（建長寺山門）[GFDL or CC BY-SA 3.0]

Wikiwikiyarou, p.13（銅鏡）[GFDL or CC BY-SA 4.0-3.0-2.5-2.0-1.0]

663highland, p.26（薬師寺）[GFDL+creative commons2.5]

まえがき

　日本の歴史を英語で語るのは、意外と難しいものです。というのも、我々がごく当たり前に使っている歴史用語や、政治や文化背景についての概念自体、海外の人には全く新しいことがらであるからです。

　例えば、「幕末」という言葉を聞いたとき、我々はペリー来航から明治維新までの動乱を漠然とでも想起できますが、海外の人のほとんどにはそれはイメージできません。坂本龍馬も西郷隆盛も聞いたことのない人物なのです。しかも幕末の「幕」の意味する徳川幕府についても同様です。

　昔、アメリカでShōgunという映画が流行り、徳川家康や「征夷大将軍」について海外でも話題になったことがありました。でもこれは例外です。

　一方で、我々が海外の人と交流するときには、常に英語で自らの国をどう解説するかという話題を「持ち駒」として大切にしておかなければなりません。しかも、歴史書の硬さをとって、できるだけシンプルに、そして明快に語れるようにしなければならないのです。

　であればこそ、自国の歴史を紹介する困難さを乗り越えて、それを世界標準の常識に照らし合わせて説明するノウハウを本書で習得していただければと思います。

　それができる人は、海外のお客様へのおもてなしに寄与できるだけではなく、海外との交流そのものを深める役割をもって活躍できるはずです。

西海コエン

目次

まえがき ………………………………………………………………… 3

第1章　日本の夜明け

1．先史時代 ……………………………………………………… 8
2．国の形成 ……………………………………………………… 12
3．大和時代 ……………………………………………………… 14
4．仏教の到来 …………………………………………………… 20

第2章　奈良時代と平安時代

5．奈良時代 ……………………………………………………… 24
6．神仏習合の時代 ……………………………………………… 28
7．源氏物語の時代 ……………………………………………… 32

第3章　中世社会

8．源氏と平家 …………………………………………………… 38
9．民衆の仏教の誕生 …………………………………………… 42
10．元寇と鎌倉幕府の崩壊 ……………………………………… 46
11．南北朝時代 …………………………………………………… 50
12．繁栄から混沌へ ……………………………………………… 54
13．戦国時代 ……………………………………………………… 56
14．西洋文化の到来 ……………………………………………… 60
15．再統一 ………………………………………………………… 64
16．豊臣秀吉とその時代 ………………………………………… 68

第4章　将軍と鎖国

17．徳川幕府の創設 ……………………………………………… 72

Contents

Chapter 1: Dawn of the Nation

1. Prehistoric Era ·· 9
2. Forming the Nation ·································· 13
3. Yamato Years ·· 15
4. Arrival of Buddhism ······························· 21

Chapter 2: Nara and Heian

5. Nara Period ·· 25
6. Era of Reconciliation between Shintoism and Buddhism ·········· 29
7. Era of *The Tale of Genji* ························ 33

Chapter 3: Medieval Society

8. The Genji and Heike ······························· 39
9. Creation of People's Buddhism ·················· 43
10. Mongolian Invasion and the Fall of Kamakura ·········· 47
11. Era of Two Imperial Courts ····················· 51
12. From Prosperity to Chaos ························· 55
13. The Warring States Period ······················· 57
14. The Advent of Western Culture ·················· 61
15. Reunification ·· 65
16. Toyotomi Hideyoshi and His Era ················ 69

Chapter 4: Shogun and Seclusion

17. Creation of the Tokugawa Shogunate ············ 73

18. 徳川幕府の基盤形成 ……………………………………… 76
19. 鎖国 ……………………………………………………… 78
20. 歌舞伎と浮世絵の時代 …………………………………… 84
21. 封建制度の衰退 …………………………………………… 88
22. 開国と倒幕 ………………………………………………… 92

第5章　明治時代

23. 明治維新 …………………………………………………… 96
24. 西南戦争から明治憲法の発布まで …………………… 100
25. 日露戦争への道 ………………………………………… 104
26. 韓国併合 ………………………………………………… 108
27. 明治時代の文化的動向 ………………………………… 112

第6章　第二次世界大戦への道

28. 大正デモクラシー ……………………………………… 116
29. 満州侵略 ………………………………………………… 120
30. 中国との戦争 …………………………………………… 124
31. 太平洋戦争と第二次世界大戦 ………………………… 128
32. 原子爆弾と日本の降伏 ………………………………… 130

第7章　グローバル・パートナーシップの時代

33. 占領と改革 ……………………………………………… 136
34. 高度経済成長とバブル経済 …………………………… 140
35. 今後の見通し …………………………………………… 146

18. The Founding of the Tokugawa Shogunate ································77
19. Closing the Nation ································79
20. The Period of Kabuki and Ukiyo-e ································85
21. Decline of the Feudal System ································89
22. Opening of the Nation and the Fall of the Tokugawa ···········93

Chapter 5: The Meiji Period

23. Meiji Restoration ································97
24. From the Seinan War to the Promulgation of the Meiji Constitution .. 101
25. Way to the Russo-Japanese War ································105
26. Annexation of Korea ································109
27. Cultural Movements in the Meiji Period ································113

Chapter 6: Path to World War II

28. Taisho Democracy ································117
29. Invasion of Manchuria ································121
30. War Against China ································125
31. The Pacific War and World War II ································129
32. The Atomic Bomb and Surrender ································131

Chapter 7: The Era of Global Partnership

33. Occupation and Reform ································137
34. Era of High Economic Growth and the Bubble Economy ········141
35. Predictions for the Future ································147

TIME LINE ································150
INDEX ································153

7

第1章 日本の夜明け

縄文時代の壺
Jomon pottery

弥生時代の壺
Yayoi pottery

1. 先史時代

　日本人はどこから来たのだろうか。この問題にはまだ明確な答えは出ていないが、日本人は単一民族である、つまり単一の人種であり単一の文化を形成するという共通認識が、日本には存在している。この見方は一つには、日本が海に囲まれており、世界の他の国々から隔離しているという事実に由来するものであるが、日本が他国と大いに対話や交流を行ってきたのも事実である。

　日本の国土は主要4島および約3,000の小さな島から成る。15,000年前の先史時代には、日本はアジアの大陸部と陸続きだった。当時大陸で見られたマンモスや、類似する動物の骨が、日本でも発見されている。

　人類がいつ日本に住むようになったかは定かではない。人類が約2万年前に南アジアや太平洋から移り渡ってきたというのが定説になっている。また、北方から来た人々もいたと考えられている。

Chapter 1:
Dawn of the Nation

1. Prehistoric Era

Where do the Japanese come from? That question is still looking for a definitive answer, but it is a common belief in Japan that the Japanese are homogeneous; that is, that they form one race and one culture. This view is partly based on the fact that Japan is surrounded by ocean and cut off from the rest of the world. Over time, however, it is true that Japan has had a good deal of interaction and exchange with the rest of the world.

Japan consists of four major islands and almost three thousand smaller islands. In prehistoric times, more than fifteen thousand years ago, Japan was geographically connected to the Asian continent. The bones of mammoths and many other animals similar to those found on the continent have been discovered in Japan.

It is uncertain when human beings first inhabited Japan. There is a widely accepted belief that people came from southern Asia and the Pacific about twenty thousand years ago. It is also thought that people came from the north.

土偶
Clay figure

9

第1章 日本の夜明け

　2,000を超える数の先史時代の出土品が日本で発見されている。紀元前8,000年より後の時代の出土品はさらに多い。この時代、人々は原始的な村に住み、狩猟や漁労に携わっていた。当時の人々は、縄目文様で飾られた粘土の壺を作っていた。

　日本語では、この縄目模様のことを「縄文」と呼んでいた。また、この時代のことを縄文時代といい、縄文時代に住んでいた人のことを縄文人と呼んでいる。

　縄文時代、日本はアジアから農業技術を少しずつ吸収した。同時期の中国では、漢字表記法をはじめさまざまな技術が開発され、他の国に伝播していた。日本も、紀元前3世紀頃に中国の文化の一部を取り入れている。

　次に到来するのが、弥生時代である。この時代には、独特の壺や土偶（粘土像）が作られた。「弥生」の名は、この時期の出土品がはじめて発見された東京近郊の遺跡に由来する。この時代には、中国の農業技術の実践など、多くの重要な発展が見られた。水田には灌漑が施され、木製、青銅製、鉄製の道具が全国的に用いられていた。弥生人は次第に縄文人が元々住んでいた地域から出ていくようになる。

弥生時代の青銅の鈴
Yayoi bronze bell

Chapter 1: Dawn of the Nation

More than two thousand prehistoric artifacts have been unearthed in Japan. Many more artifacts date from after circa 8,000 B.C. During this time, life was characterized by primitive villages of hunters and fishermen. The people of this time made clay pots decorated with cord markings. The Japanese word for these cord designs is *jomon*, which is also the name given to the period and to the people living in Japan at that time.

During the Jomon Period, the Japanese gradually imported farming skills from the rest of Asia. At the same time, in China, the Chinese writing system and many other technologies were developed and spread to other countries. The Japanese also adopted certain aspects of Chinese culture around the third century B.C.

The Yayoi Period is the next era, which is characterized by its distinctive pottery and clay figures. The name "Yayoi" derives from the archeological site near Tokyo where artifacts from the period were first uncovered. There were many important developments during this time, including the implementation of Chinese agricultural techniques. Rice fields were irrigated, and wooden, bronze, and iron tools were used throughout the country. Over time, the Yayoi people largely displaced the original Jomon inhabitants.

ヒスイまたはメノウから作られた牙状のアクセサリー

Fang-shaped accessories made from jade or agate

2. 国の形成

　大陸の影響は古代日本の政治文化史における中核的な要素であったことは言うまでもないが、日本が一つの国として統一された過程について、正確なことは分かっていない。現代の日本人は、アジア大陸から三々五々と日本へと渡来した人々の子孫である可能性が高い。渡来人たちは、中国の影響を受けた、比較的洗練された技術を身につけていた。

　中国は紀元前221年に統一されて、清朝による統治が始まった。イエス＝キリストが世に現れた時代に、中国は勢力を大いに拡大し、ローマ帝国に比肩しうる存在となっていた。中国のような影響力の強い権力中枢と、朝鮮や日本のような比較的弱小の村落や部族との間に多くの交流があったであろうことは想像に難くない。

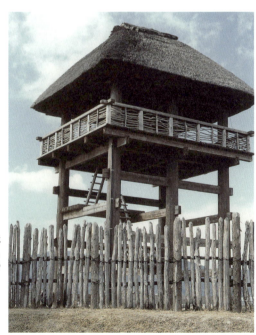

佐賀県吉野ヶ里遺跡における弥生時代の物見櫓の復元建物。吉野ヶ里遺跡は、紀元前3世紀から紀元3世紀頃のものと考えられている

Reconstruction of Yayoi watch-tower at Yoshinogari site, Saga pref. Yoshinogari dates to between the third century B.C. and the third century A.D.

2. Forming the Nation

While continental Asian influence was undeniably a pivotal element in the political and cultural history of ancient Japan, it is still unclear exactly how the Japanese were united as one nation. Modern Japanese may well be the descendants of continental Asian peoples that came to Japan in waves, one after the other. They had relatively sophisticated technologies that were influenced by the Chinese.

China was united around 221 B.C. when the Qin Dynasty and a new imperial government were established. Around the time of Jesus Christ, China greatly expanded its reach, becoming somewhat like the Roman Empire. One can easily imagine that there would be many interactions between an influential center of power such as China and the relatively weaker villages and tribes of Korea and Japan.

弥生時代の青銅鏡。宗教的儀式に用いられたと考えられている

Yayoi bronze mirror thought to be used in religious rituals

中国の影響により、部族の中にはさらに強力な政治組織を作り出すものもあった。日本の使者が漢の宮廷を訪れた最初の記録は紀元57年であるが、朝鮮や日本で国家の形成に向けた動きが最初に見られるのは、3世紀になってからのことである。

この時期、卑弥呼という日本の神秘的な預言者のことが中国の史書に記されている。卑弥呼は邪馬台国を統べる女王であり、中国の魏の宮廷と接触したとされており、日本人は法を守り、社会の秩序を重んじる民族であると書かれている。人々は農業や漁業、あるいは紡績や織物業を営んでいた。史書にはさらに、古代日本の統治者たちは男性であったことも女性であったこともあったと記している。

邪馬台国の都の場所については、考古学者の間で今なお争いがある。九州説を唱える学者もいれば、京都の南、大和地方説を支持する学者もある。初めの都は九州だったと思われるが、古い伝承によると、一世紀後になって、有力な氏族であった大和民族が大和地方への移住を決めて、初の朝廷を築いたとされている。

3. 大和時代

日本では長らく、天皇を神と崇めてきた。今日ではもちろん、天皇制はイギリスの王室に近い存在になっている。天皇は単に国民の象徴であると考えられ、皇室には政治的権力がない。

The Chinese impact stimulated some of these tribes to create more powerful political organizations. The very first recorded visit of a Japanese envoy to the Han court was in 57 A.D. However, the first movements toward creating nations in Korea and Japan probably did not begin until the third century.

During this time, the mysterious Japanese prophetess Himiko was mentioned in Chinese historical records. The records say she was the queen of the Yamatai kingdom, which had contact with the court of the Wei Dynasty in China. The Japanese are described in these records as being law-abiding people who paid close attention to social hierarchies. They practiced agriculture and fishing, as well as spinning and weaving. The records further note that the rulers of the early Japanese were sometimes male and sometimes female.

Still today, archeologists argue about where Yamatai's capital was located. Some say it was in Kyushu, while others believe it was in the Yamato area, south of Kyoto. While the original capital may indeed have been in Kyushu, early legends suggest that, a century later, the predominant Yamato clan decided to move to the Yamato area where the first government was formed.

3. Yamato Years

Japan long regarded the emperor as being divine. Today, of course, the imperial system is more like the system of the United Kingdom. The emperor is seen as merely a symbol of the nation, and the imperial court has no political power.

第1章 日本の夜明け

　しかし、第二次世界大戦までは状況が異なっていた。歴史の始まりから1945年まで、日本人は万世一系の皇室の伝統に従い、それを尊重してきた。天皇は日本の文化に大きな影響を与えたが、政治に常に関与したわけではなく、武士階級が政治権力を握ることも多かった。

　強力な朝廷がはじめて形成されたのは、3世紀終わり頃のことである。これは、大和地方に設立されたため、大和朝廷と呼ばれた。大和地方は京都の南に位置し、紀伊半島の中央まで伸びている。強力な政府が出現した経緯については十分には明らかでないが、し烈な権力争いを経て誕生したものと見られている。

　この権力闘争は、朝鮮半島の政治動向とも関連があった。中国における当時の史書によると、朝鮮半島の王国間の戦いにおいて、日本は百済国に援軍を派遣するように要請されている。百済国は朝鮮半島の南西にあった王国である。391年、日本は北方にあった高句麗国との大きな戦いに援軍を送っている。

　この事例から、興味深い仮説が生じる。つまり、日本の皇族は、かつて日本の国土を侵略した朝鮮人の子孫だったのではないだろうか、という仮説である。これが事実なら、天皇が朝鮮に援軍を送ったのは自らの権益を守るためだったのかもしれない。

　あるいは、日本人は朝鮮半島を征服するために軍勢を結集して派遣したのかもしれない。考古学者や人類学者、歴史学者たちの間では、実際には何が起こったのか、あるいはなぜ起こったのかについて、今日なお多くの仮説が見られる。

　4世紀末以降、日本人は時折朝鮮半島に政治的関心や領土的野心を抱くようになる。しかし662年、中国の海軍が新

The situation was different until the end of World War II. From the beginnings of their history until 1945 the Japanese followed and respected the same imperial tradition. The emperor had great influence on Japanese culture, although not always in politics, where the warrior class was often paramount.

A strong imperial government was first formed around the end of the third century A.D. It is referred to as the Yamato Imperial Court, because it was located in the region called Yamato. This region is south of Kyoto and extends to the center of the Kii Peninsula. Although it is not entirely clear how such a strong government came into being, it seems to have been forged through an intense power struggle.

This power struggle was related to political movements on the Korean Peninsula. According to Chinese histories of the time, the Japanese were asked to send troops to help support Paekche (Kudara in Japanese) during the battles between Korean kingdoms. Paekche is located in the southwest part of the Korean Peninsula. In the year 391, Japanese troops fought a major battle with Koguryo (Kokuri), the kingdom to the north.

This event suggests an intriguing possibility—namely, whether the Japanese imperial clan originated, in fact, in Korean peoples that invaded Japanese soil in earlier years. If this is true, it might be that the Japanese emperor sent troops to Korea to protect his own interests. Or did the Japanese unite and marshal their forces with a view to conquering the Korean Peninsula. Many hypotheses are still heard today among archaeologists, anthropologists, and historians as to what actually happened and why.

Since the end of the fourth century, the Japanese would, from time to time, reveal their political and territorial interest in Korea. In 662 the Chinese navy effectively stifled that interest by defeating the Japanese

第1章 日本の夜明け

羅（朝鮮半島西部にあった王国）を支援して日本の海軍を打ち負かし、日本の野望を見事に打ち砕いた。

こうした一連の戦いから、有史時代の最初より日本はアジア大陸に深く関わっていたことが分かる。古代の日本は、国内の動向を通じて自らのアイデンティティを形成したわけではない。むしろ朝鮮や、やはり朝鮮半島に力を及ぼそうとしていた中国との意識的な関わりを通じてアイデンティティを確立してきたのである。

実際、日本に朝廷が出現した時代には、多くの朝鮮人や中国人が日本に来て、朝廷や有力豪族に仕え、国の発展に尽くした。渡来人たちは技術に加えて漢字をもたらした。漢字は優れた表記体系であり、日本はこの体系を採用した。また、多くの歴代天皇は中国に使節を遣わし、中国政府と経済、文化、政治面での交流を行った。

大和政権の強大さは、古墳に見て取ることができる。3世紀から5世紀にかけて、皇室や豪族は日本各地に巨大な古墳を作った。その多くは大和地方やその周辺に見られる。最も巨大な古墳は、5世紀の仁徳天皇陵である。鍵穴型が特徴の仁徳天皇陵は、世界最大級の墓である。

5世紀から6世紀にかけて、大和に拠点を定めた歴代天皇は日本全土に影響力を及ぼした。唯一力が及ばなかった地域は、本州北部と北海道である。これらの地域は、さまざまな部族が支配しており、日本とは別の国と考えられていた。

鍵穴型の仁徳天皇陵（4世紀）。世界最大級の墓

Keyhole-shaped burial mound for the Emperor Nintoku (fourth century), one of the biggest for its size in the world

navy and supporting Shilla (Shiragi), the kingdom in the western part of the Korean Peninsula.

This series of battles indicates that Japan was deeply involved with the Asian continent from the beginning of its recorded history. Japan did not, in fact, take its early identity from any domestic initiative. It took it from the consciousness of its connections with Korea and even China, which was also interested in influencing the Korean Peninsula.

In fact, when the Japanese imperial government was formed, thousands of Koreans and Chinese came to Japan, to be hired by the government and powerful local leaders and contribute to the country's development. In addition to technology, they also brought *kanji*, or Chinese characters, a sophisticated writing system that the Japanese adopted. Also, many Japanese emperors sent delegations to China to create economic, cultural, and political interactions with the Chinese government.

The power of the Yamato government can be seen in their *kofun*, or burial mounds. Between the third and fifth centuries, the imperial family and strong local leaders created huge *kofun* throughout Japan, most of which were centered in the Yamato region and surrounding areas. The most massive was that built in the fifth century for Emperor Nintoku. With a distinctive key-hole shape, it is one of the largest tombs in the world.

From the fifth century and into the sixth, Yamato emperors established their influence throughout Japan. The only areas they didn't influence were the northern part of Honshu and Hokkaido. These areas were considered almost separate nations with different tribes of people.

4. 仏教の到来

　仏教は、主に中国や朝鮮の僧侶を通じて、6世紀中頃に日本に到来した。仏教は単なる宗教や哲学にとどまらず、独特の国際的な文明でもあった。当時の学者や知識人でもあった僧侶たちは、価値ある実用的な文化をもたらした。医療技術や灌漑、さらには世界観までもが、彼らによって伝えられた。

　今日、仏教寺院は日本のいたるところにある。だから、日本の歴史が始まって以来、仏教は日本の文化にとって重要であったと考える人もいるかもしれない。しかし実際はそうではない。仏教はむしろ、6世紀における国際化の象徴であると考えることができる。

　ゴータマ・シッダールタがこの国際的な宗教を創設した後、日本に伝播するまで1,000年の時を要した。その間、仏教は他の文化や宗教とも接触していた。たとえば、アレキサンダー大王が中央アジアに遠征し、ギリシア文化が仏教と接する契機となった。もちろん、インドで確立した仏教は、古代インド文明の影響を大いに受けている。また、中国、東南アジアおよび朝鮮へと、徐々に東方へと伝播するに従って、他の多くの要素が仏教の形成に影響を与えた。そのため、仏教が最終的に日本に到来したときには、その独特な宗教だけではなく、国際的な世界観など、他の恩恵ももたらしたのである。

　しかし、仏教は日本にとってはまったく新しい宗教であり、日本固有の文化とは大いに異なっていたため、日本人の生活に与える影響に懸念を有する者もいた。彼らは仏教を、外国文明の侵略のようなもので、破壊的な影響をもたらしかねないものであると考えたのである。実際、この懸

4. Arrival of Buddhism

Buddhism first came to Japan in the middle of the sixth century, principally through the medium of Chinese and Korean priests. Buddhism was not only a religion and a philosophy; it was also a distinctive, cosmopolitan civilization. The priests, who were the scholars and intellectuals of the time, brought valuable practical culture with them. This included medical technology and irrigation, along with their worldview.

飛鳥寺の大仏
Daibutsu at the Asuka-dera

Buddhist temples are everywhere in Japan today. One might think that Buddhism was an important part of Japanese culture from the very beginning of its history. But that is not the case. In fact, Buddhism could be considered the sixth-century symbol of internationalization.

After Siddhartha Gautama created this cosmopolitan religion, it took 1,000 years to reach Japan. During that time, Buddhism came in contact with other cultures and religions. For example, the expedition of Alexander the Great to Central Asia brought Greek culture into contact with Buddhism. Of course, with its establishment in India, Buddhism had considerable influences from ancient Indian civilization. Many other influences helped shape Buddhism as it gradually moved eastward through China, Southeast Asia, and Korea. Thus, when Buddhism finally arrived in Japan, it brought not only a distinctive religion but other benefits, including its cosmopolitan view of the world.

However, Buddhism was very new to Japan and very different from its indigenous culture. Some people were concerned about its influence on Japanese life. They thought Buddhism might have a distrupting impact, much like the invasion of an alien civilization. Indeed, this concern created serious political conflict among the powerful clans of

第1章 日本の夜明け

念は朝廷における有力豪族同士の深刻な政治的紛争をもたらした。この争いに終止符が打たれたのは、仏教を信奉する蘇我氏が対立する物部氏を下した587年のことである。

蘇我氏が台頭した時代、仏教は大和朝廷の庇護の下で広く浸透した。この時期、聖徳太子が推古天皇の摂政として実権を掌握していた。聖徳太子は中国の隋と正式な外交関係を樹立し、遣隋使と呼ばれる使節団を派遣した。この使節派遣は10世紀初めまで続くこととなり、この制度を通じて数百人にのぼる学生が中国に留学した。

聖徳太子は、有名な十七条から成る、日本初の憲法を制定したことでも知られている。彼の治世は、朝廷が置かれた場所にちなんで飛鳥時代と呼ばれる。飛鳥時代は日本で最も早期の仏教文化と関連している。現存する世界最古の木造建築である法隆寺もこの時代に建立されている。同寺の建築や彫刻からは、外国の影響を多大に受けていたことが窺える。

聖徳太子が622年に亡くなると、蘇我氏と対抗勢力との抗争が始まった。その後645年には、中大兄皇子が中臣鎌足の助力を得て、蘇我一族の長であった蘇我入鹿を暗殺する。このクーデターを皮切りに、大化の改新と呼ばれる朝廷の全面的な改革が始まった。

新政府は、中国の制度をモデルとして権力を強化した。主な改善点は、登録制度を通じた実効性のある税収管理であった。中大兄皇子は668年に即位して天智天皇となり、672年に退位する前に、官僚制度や法制度を刷新した。朝廷は、国の安定のために仏教哲学や宗教的権威を利用した。

聖徳太子(574–622)と二人の息子
Prince Shotoku (574–622) with his two sons

the imperial government. This struggle came to an end in 587 A.D., when the Soga clan, which supported Buddhism, defeated the opposing Mononobe clan.

During the era of the Soga clan's ascendancy, Buddhism was widely accepted under the auspices of the Yamato imperial government. Prince Shotoku established his leadership at this time as regent to the Empress Suiko. He began an official diplomatic relationship with the Sui Dynasty of China and sent envoys called *kenzuishi*. This envoy system continued to the beginning of the tenth century. Through it, hundreds of student were sent to study in China.

Prince Shotoku is also known as the creator of Japan's first constitution, with its renowned seventeen articles. His era is called the Asuka Period and was named after the location of the government. The Asuka Period is associated with the earliest Buddhist culture in Japan. Horyu-ji temple, the oldest wooden structure in the world, was built during this time. Its architecture and sculptures reveal a great amount of influence from other countries.

After the death of Prince Shotoku in 622, a power struggle began between the Soga and rival clans. Eventually, in 645, Prince Nakano-oe (or Nakano-oe no Oji), who was supported by Nakatomi no Kamatari, assassinated Soga no Iruka, head of the Soga clan. This coup d'état started a complete reformation of the imperial government, which was called the Taika Reform.

The new government consolidated its power based on the Chinese model. The main change was to implement effective tax management through a registry system. Prince Nakano-oe became Emperor Tenji in 668. Before leaving the throne in 672, he had established a new bureaucracy and legal system. The imperial government utilized Buddhist philosophy and religious power to stabilize the country.

第2章 奈良時代と平安時代

5. 奈良時代

　7世紀も終わる頃に薬師寺が日本で建立されたが、当時中国では唐王朝が勃興していた。唐は世界史の中でも最も繁栄を極めた帝国の一つであり、その領土は、中東の東端にまで及んでいた。中東では、東西の文化交流が盛んに行われていたが、これは一つには、中国の西隣の国家がイスラム帝国であり、その影響力が西ヨーロッパに及んでいたことによる。実際、中国とイスラム帝国は、世界をリードする二大文明であり、当時の最先端のテクノロジーを手中に収めていた。

　中国とイスラム帝国との交易路はシルクロードと呼ばれていた。無数の商人や僧侶、学者、そして兵士らがこの道を通った。中国から西洋に製紙の技法がもたらされたのも、この道を通じてである。これは、651年にイスラム軍が唐軍に勝利した後のことであり、マルコ・ポーロは600年後にこの道を歩くことになる。シルクロードは、西端はスペイン、東端は日本にまで及んでいた。

　聖徳太子の時代から9世紀初頭まで、日本は中国やその国際的な文明に多大な影響を受けていた。朝廷は大宝律令という法を制定した。大宝律令は法的問題や税、社会階級、軍、および政治制度について定めている。

Chapter 2:
Nara and Heian

5. Nara Period

When Yakushi-ji temple was built in Japan near the end of the seventh century, China was in the early stages of the Tang Dynasty. Tang China was one of the most prosperous empires in world history, its territory reaching as far as the eastern edges of the Middle East. In the Middle East, there was much exchange between eastern and western cultures. This was due in part to the fact that China's western neighbor at the time was the Saracen Empire, the influence of which reached as far as western Europe. In fact, China and the Saracens were the world's two leading civilizations, boasting the most advanced technology of the time.

The trade route between China and the Saracens was called the Silk Road. Countless merchants, monks, students, and soldiers traveled this road. It was the path along which the art of paper-making came to the West from China. This happened after the Saracen army defeated the Tang army in 651 A.D. Marco Polo was to travel along this route six hundred years later. The Silk Road stretched as far west as Italy and Spain and as far east as Japan.

Between Prince Shotoku's era and the beginning of the ninth century, Japan was greatly influenced by China and its cosmopolitan civilization. The imperial government established a law called the Taiho Constitution. This law covered legal matters, tax, social class, the military, and the political system.

第2章 奈良時代と平安時代

　元明天皇が710年に奈良への遷都を決定した際、日本は既に高度な政府や法制度を備えていた。奈良の都を設計するに当たり、天皇は碁盤目状に整然と区分けされた唐の首都長安をモデルとした。710年から784年までの時代を奈良時代と呼ぶ。

　奈良時代は、きわめて活発な時代だった。多くの使節が唐の都に派遣された。中国に学んだ多くの留学生たちが日本に戻って、重要な政治的役割を担った。またこの時期に、日本初の通貨が流通した。

　奈良時代は、仏教が日本の政治に影響を与え始めた時代としても知られている。聖武天皇は、仏教を崇拝すれば反乱や自然災害などの国家の危機も防ぐことができると信じていた。そこで聖武天皇は、大仏像を都に作るよう命じた。この大仏は現在、奈良の東大寺で見ることができる。東大寺では、中国やインド、中東由来のさまざまな楽器や壺、装飾品を収めた宝物殿（正倉院）もよく知られている。

薬師寺。680年頃、現在の奈良市郊外に建立された
Yakushi-ji temple, erected around 680 A.D. in the suburbs of current Nara city

When the Empress Gemmei decided to move the capital to Nara in 710, Japan already had a sophisticated government and legal system. When the city of Nara was designed, the grid pattern of Chang'an, the Tang Dynasty capital, served as a model. The era between 710 and 784 is called the Nara Period.

The Nara Period was an eminently active era. Numerous envoys were dispatched to the Tang court. Many students sent to study in China returned to Japan to play important governmental roles. Japan circulated its first currency during this time.

The Nara Period is also known as the era when Buddhism started to influence Japanese politics. Emperor Shomu believed that if Buddhism was revered, national crises such as rebellions and natural disasters could be prevented. Thus, he ordered a huge statue of Buddha to be built in the capital. This statue can be seen today in Todai-ji temple in Nara. Todai-ji is also known for its treasure house, the Shoso-in, a repository of a variety of musical instruments, pottery, and decorative arts that came from China, India, and the Middle East.

東大寺。大仏像で知られる、奈良時代を代表する寺
Todai-ji temple, the iconic temple of the Nara Period with its gigantic statue of Buddha

天皇が仏教を信奉したことにより、僧侶が権力を掌握し、中央政府に影響力を及ぼし始めた。これにより、聖武天皇の死後に政治的混乱が生じた。最初の問題は、東大寺の建設のために百姓に課された重税と、それにより生活に悪影響が生じたことであった。

奈良時代はまた、日本初の史書である古事記や日本書紀が記された時代でもあった。古事記は日本古代の神話についての物語であり、日本書紀は大和時代の歴史を記述している。奈良時代の最も有名な出版物は、759年以降のある時点に編纂された和歌集である万葉集であろう。奈良時代は、桓武天皇が今日の京都郊外にある長岡京への遷都を決めた784年に終わりを告げた。

6. 神仏習合の時代

長岡京は、政争のために完成前に放棄され、794年に平安京へと再び遷都が行われた。平安京は今日京都と呼ばれており、794年から1192年までを平安時代という。平安京は、奈良と同じく唐の首都長安をモデルにして設計された。平安時代の前期は奈良時代と同じくアジアの影響を多大に受けており、中国や朝鮮、渤海（満州とシベリア東部にまたがっていた王国）との交易も行われていた。

Imperial support of Buddhism afforded Buddhist monks a position of power, and they began to exert influence on the central government. In the end this led to political turmoil after the death of Emperor Shomu. The first problem was the heavy taxes levied on farmers to build Todai-ji and the negative impact in had on their lives.

Nara was also the era in which Japan's first historical documents, *Kojiki* (Records of Ancient Matters) and *Nihonshoki* (The Chronicles of Japan), were published. *Kojiki* narrates the mythology of ancient Japan. *Nihonshoki* tells the history of the Yamato era. The most notable Nara publication was the *Man'yoshu* (Collection of Myriad Leaves), an anthology of poetry compiled sometime after 759. The Nara era came to an end in 784 when Emperor Kammu decided to move the capital to Nagaoka, in the suburbs of present-day Kyoto.

6. Era of Reconciliation between Shintoism and Buddhism

The Nagaoka capital was abandoned before it was even completed owing to political strife, to be relocated again to Heian-kyo in 794. Today Heian-kyo is known as Kyoto. The period of time from that date until 1192 is known as the Heian Period. Heian-kyo, like Nara, was modeled after the capital of the Tang Dynasty, Chang'an. The early part of the Heian Period was similar to the Nara Period, with a great deal of Asian influence. There were trade relationships with China, Korea, and Balhae (Bokkai in Japanese), a kingdom located in Manchuria and eastern Siberia.

第2章 奈良時代と平安時代

9世紀初め、2名の僧侶、最澄と空海が中国から戻り、新しい仏教の宗派である天台宗と真言宗を創始した。二つの宗派はいずれも強い影響力を持つこととなった。その哲学は難解で、僧侶たちが教義を理解するには長年の研鑽と修行を要した。多くの寺は山奥に建てられており、僧侶たちは世俗とは切り離された生活を送っていた。

次第に、これらの新しい宗派は日本土着の宗教と混合して、一連の新しい宗教的慣わしが生まれた。日本人は伝統的に神（精霊）が自然に宿っていると信じており、山や滝、湖、石や木を、精霊が具現化したものとして崇めていた。こうした信仰が時とともに発展して儀式となった。こうした儀式が神道、つまり「神の道」という宗教となった。

神道は皇族の宗教であると考えられることが多い。これはある意味では正しい。皇族と深い関わりのある神社は数多くある。その典型は大和時代初期に建立された伊勢神宮である。しかし古代では、それぞれの地域で自然の精霊に対する信仰が見られ、こうした各地域の宗教ものちに神社

平安京のモデル
Model of Heian-kyo

At the beginning of the ninth century, the priests Saicho and Kukai returned from China and started two new Buddhist sects, the Tendai and Shingon, both of which became very influential. Their philosophical theories were steeped in complexity, and monks had to study and train for years to master them. Many temples were built deep in the mountains, where monks lived lives cut off from the mundane world.

Gradually, these new Buddhist sects mingled with the local Japanese religions and created a new set of religious practices. Traditionally, Japanese believed that *kami*, or spirits, were inherent in nature. Mountains, waterfalls, lakes, stones and trees were respected as embodying those spirits. This belief developed over time and became ritualized. These rituals became the religion known as Shinto, or the "Way of the Gods."

Shinto is often seen as the religion of the imperial family. That is partly true. There are many Shinto shrines deeply related to the imperial family. A typical example is Ise Shrine, which was built in the early part of the Yamato era. However, every local region had its own beliefs in the spirits of nature. These local religions later erected shrines to show

熊野神社の旧大社である大斎原の入口に立つ大鳥居

The huge torii gate at the entrance to the funeral facilities where Kumano Shrine once stood

を建立し、神への信仰を表現していた。19世紀末には、こうした地域の宗教も神道として公式に統合されていった。

　9世紀になると、上に見た仏教の新宗派は神道の慣わしを取り入れ始めた。たとえば、仏教の僧侶たちは、お祓いのような神道の各種儀式を取り入れて、自然に対する敬意を表し始めた。こうしたプロセスを経て、仏教は平安時代において国家の宗教として認められていった。

　儀式や一定の形式により敬意を示すやり方は、実業界をはじめ、現代の日本にも残っている。たとえば、名刺交換や、神職が新しい建物の建設現場で地鎮祭を行ったりするときに、こうした儀式が見られる。株式取引所が年末に取引を終了する際の特別な慣わし（大納会）もその一例である。このような儀式や伝統的な営みは、日本でビジネスを行う上で現在でもとても大切なものであると考えられている。

7. 源氏物語の時代

　仏教の僧侶たちが神道を取り入れたことは、外国文化の「国風化」のプロセスの一環であった。これは日本史全体に見られる傾向であるが、平安時代はその格好の例である。中国では唐王朝が没落し、907年についに滅びた。その後中国では内戦を経て、960年に宋が出現する。これにより中国との関係が途絶えた日本は、中国の文化を吸収して完全に国風のものに変える余裕を得た。これにより、日本は独自の文化を確立できるようになった。

respect for their *kami*. In the late nineteenth century, these regional religions were officially unified as Shintoism.

During the ninth century, the new Buddhist sects began to adopt Shinto practices. For example, Buddhist monks began to show their respect for nature with various Shinto rites, such as purification. Through this process, Buddhism was eventually recognized as the national religion during the Heian Period.

Showing respect through rituals or established forms has persisted into modern Japan, including the Japanese business world. These practices can be seen, for example, when business cards are exchanged, or when a Shinto priest recites prayers at the construction site of a new building. It is also seen in the special way the stock exchange is closed at the end of every year. Such rituals and conventional acts are still thought to be quite important to doing business in Japan.

7. Era of *The Tale of Genji*

The adaptation of Shintoism by Buddhists was part of a process of "Japanizing" foreign culture. This has been a trend throughout Japan's history, and the Heian Period offers an excellent example. In China, the Tang Dynasty was collapsing and finally succumbed in 907. Civil war was followed by the emergence of the Song Dynasty in 960. This led to a lapse in connections with China and gave Japan the leeway to absorb Chinese culture and transform it into something thoroughly Japanese. This process eventually helped Japan establish its own cultural identity.

このプロセスの一環で、日本人は中国の漢字を受け入れて簡略化し、独自の表記体系を作り上げた。その結果、中国の漢字と、平仮名や片仮名という表音文字を混合した表記が生まれた。この体系を用いて、日本人は小説や和歌、随筆を数多く生み出した。

　こうした文学作品のうち最もよく知られているのは、11世紀初頭に成立した紫式部の「源氏物語」だろう。この長編恋愛小説は、世界最初の小説と考える人が多い。平安時代は、文学が大いに創作された時代だった。最上の作品の中には、貴族階級の娘や妻、愛人たちであった女性の手によるものが見られた。源氏物語で描かれた世界は、朝廷とそこに住む貴族たちの生活を俯瞰している。

　平安時代に政治的権力を掌握したのは藤原氏だった。藤原氏は645年に大化の改新で重要な役割を演じた中臣鎌足の子孫である。藤原氏は経済と政治、両面の戦略で権力を保持した。日本全土の広大な田畑を支配するとともに、皇族

紫式部
Murasaki Shikibu

源氏物語「若紫」
The Tale of Genji,
"Young Murasaki"

One example of this process is how the Japanese adopted Chinese characters, making many of them simpler and creating their own writing system. The resultant system was a mixture of Chinese characters and the phonetic systems *hiragana* and *katakana*. Using this system, the Japanese created a rich variety of novels, poems and essays.

Perhaps the best known of these literary works is Lady Murasaki's *Genji Monogatari*, or "The Tale of Genji," which was brought to completion at the beginning of the eleventh century. This great love story is considered by many to be the world's first novel. Indeed, the Heian Period was a time of great literary creativity. Some of the best writing was done by women who were the daughters, wives, and mistresses of aristocrats. The world described in *The Tale of Genji* encompasses the life of the imperial court and its aristocratic inhabitants.

The principal political power in the Heian Period was the Fujiwara clan. They were the descendants of Nakatomi no Kamatari, who played an important role in the Taika Reform of 645. The Fujiwara clan held

源氏物語「匂宮」
The Tale of Genji, "His Perfumed Highness"

との婚姻を通じて影響力を行使したのである。しかし、藤原氏の奢侈な生活は朝廷の不興を買った。さらに藤原氏が栄華を謳歌していた頃、地方では新たな動きが生じつつあったのである。

　奈良時代から平安時代前期にかけては、全ての土地が国家に属していた。しかし、重大な例外が一つあった。新しく開墾された地方の土地は、私有が認められたのである。このため、藤原氏や有力寺院は地方で新しい土地の開墾に大いに投資した。その結果、大宝律令により確立した朝廷の徴税制度は次第に崩壊した。私有の荘園を守り、荘園から徴税するために、藤原氏をはじめとする有力貴族や寺院は武士と呼ばれる侍を雇用してその任に当たらせた。10世紀半ば頃、武士の多くは源氏と平家という日本の二大武家に忠誠を誓っていた。

　1086年、数回の政争を経て、藤原氏は朝廷で獲得した政治的権力を皇族に返還した。しかし、政治経済をめぐる状況は悪化していた。それは、天皇も藤原氏と同様の経済的圧力を受けていたからである。天皇も政府の安全と安定のために武士を必要としていた。こうした強力な武士階級が、朝廷や貴族社会を変容していったのである。

its power by two main strategies—economic and political. The clan controlled large areas of farmland throughout Japan. They also gained influence through marriages with the emperor's family. However, their extravagant lifestyle eventually created dissatisfaction in the imperial court. Indeed, while the Fujiwara clan was enjoying its prosperity, a new movement was looming in the rural areas.

In both the Nara and early part of the Heian Period, all land belonged to the nation. There was one important exception, however. Rural land that was newly cultivated could be privately owned. For this reason, the Fujiwara clan and powerful temples invested heavily in cultivating new land in the provinces. As a consequence, the imperial tax system that had been established with the Taiho Constitution gradually collapsed. In order to protect their private estates and to collect taxes from them, the Fujiwara and other powerful aristocrats and temples hired professional samurai, called *bushi*, to do their bidding. Around the middle of the tenth century, many of these warriors owed allegiance to two of the most powerful clans in the country, the Genji and Heike.

In 1086, after several military set-tos, the Fujiwara clan returned the political power it had gained in the imperial court to the imperial family. On the other hand, however, the economic and political situation worsened. The reason for this lies in the fact that the emperor was more or less subject to the same economic pressures as the Fujiwara clan. In fact, he also needed professional warriors to keep the government safe and stable. Thus it was that these powerful warrior clans began to transform the imperial court and aristocratic society.

第3章 中世社会

8. 源氏と平家

　12世紀の中頃までには、武士が日本の政治において重要な役割を果たし始めていた。対立する二つの氏族、源氏と平家は、1159年から1185年まで覇権を争った。彼らの戦いはしばしば源平合戦と呼ばれる。

　当初は、平清盛の主導により平家が優勢であったが、後に平家は、源氏によって決定的な一連の敗戦を喫することとなった。平家の戦いについては、平家物語という叙事詩に記述されている。この長編物語を誰が書いたのかは明らかになっていない。諸国を巡る僧が琵琶を弾きながら、この叙事詩を長く語り伝えてきた。

　平家の崩壊後、源氏の大将であった源頼朝が征夷大将軍（最高位の将軍、すなわち大将軍）に任命され、国の事実上の指導者となった。頼朝は、1192年、鎌倉に武家政権、すなわち幕府を開いた。これは、国内に政府が二か所存在することを意味し、京都の朝廷において相当な不満を引き起こした。この不満は、第三代将軍源実朝の暗殺で頂点に達した。

　暗殺を仕掛けたのは、頼朝の妻の一族である北条氏であった。陰謀が成功すると、

源頼朝。日本の歴史上、武家政権における最初の指導者（将軍）

Minamoto no Yoritomo, the first leader (shogun) of a military government in Japanese history

Chapter 3:
Medieval Society

壇ノ浦の戦い。源平合戦の最終決戦
Battle of Dan-no ura. The final stage of the Gempei War

8. The Genji and Heike

By the mid-twelfth century, samurai had begun to play a major role in Japanese politics. Two rival clans, the Genji and the Heike, battled for dominance between 1159 and 1185. Their struggle is often referred to as the Gempei War.

In the beginning, the Heike clan emerged preeminent under the leadership of Taira no Kiyomori. Later, it suffered a series of decisive defeats at the hands of the Genji. The Heike's struggles are described in the epic literary work *Heike Monogatari*, or *The Tale of Heike*. Nobody knows who wrote this lengthy narrative. Its lyrics were long sung by traveling monks to the accompaniment of a *biwa*, or Japanese lute.

After the fall of the Heike, the Genji commander Minamoto no Yoritomo was appointed shogun (supreme general or generalissimo) and became the effective leader of the country. Yoritomo established his military government, or shogunate, in Kamakura in 1192. This meant there were two seats of government in the country, causing considerable frustration at the imperial court in Kyoto. This frustration came to a head in the assassination of the third shogun, Minamoto no Sanetomo.

The instigator of the assassination was the family of Yoritomo's wife, the Hojo clan. After the success of their plot, the Hojo assumed

第3章 中世社会

　北条氏は、将軍の代理を務める執権として幕府の主導権を握った。1221年、朝廷の軍が、実朝の暗殺に続く鎌倉の政変に乗じて攻撃を開始したが、幕府の勢力に打ち勝つことはできなかった。

　その後、天皇は日本社会の最高位の象徴として尊敬され続けたが、事実上の行政権は将軍の手中にあった。この体制は、1868年に明治維新が近代の政治形態をもたらすまで、さまざまな形で続いた。

　幕府の設立と同時期に、広く社会において重大な文化的変革が起きた。それは、身分や学問を称賛することから、武士に備わっている忠義と名誉に尊敬を払うことへの段階的な変化であった。「武士道」は、武士に求められる勇気、義務、自己犠牲の理想を説明する語である。この考え方は、日本人の心理に深く染み込み、今日に至るまで、日本社会のさまざまな側面に表れている。

鎌倉の鶴岡八幡宮
Tsurugaoka Hachiman Shrine, Kamakura

leadership of the shogunate as regents acting on behalf of the shogun. Hoping to take advantage of political turmoil in Kamakura following Sanetomo's assassination, the imperial army launched an attack in 1221, but failed to overcome the shogunate forces.

Subsequently, although the emperor continued to be respected as the highest figure in Japanese society, executive powers were actually in the hands of the shogun. This system, in various forms, lasted until 1868, when the Meiji Restoration ushered in a modern form of government.

The establishment of a shogunate coincided with an important cultural shift in wider society. That is, a gradual transition from admiration of the gentleman and the scholar to a new respect for loyalty and honor among samurai. Bushido, "the code of the warrior," delineates the ideals of courage, duty, and self-sacrifice expected of a samurai. This way of thinking became deeply ingrained in Japanese psychology, and to this day it is evident in various aspects of Japanese society.

9. 民衆の仏教の誕生

　鎌倉時代 (1185–1333) には、新しい仏教の宗派が多数誕生した。特に重要だったのは浄土宗である。浄土宗は、10世紀に浄土教として始まり、法然上人のもとで浄土宗として知られるようになった。1224年には、親鸞聖人によって浄土真宗としてさらに発展した。

　浄土真宗の中心となる信条は、念仏の「南無阿弥陀仏」を繰り返し唱えれば、阿弥陀の無限の慈悲によって死後に救われるという考えであった。さらに浄土真宗では、この世は幻のようなもので、何人も何物も永久には続かない、よって、念仏をただ信じて唱えることが死後の救済を意味すると信じられていた。浄土真宗は、その分かりやすい信条から、非常に普及した。また浄土真宗は、戦争、病気、貧困により社会が不安定だった時代の要求にも応えた。

　13世紀に日蓮上人によって誕生した別の宗派である日蓮宗では、仏教の重要な経典である法華経の読誦を中心にしていた。排他主義者の日蓮は、自らの信念ややり方に従わない他の宗派を批判した。日蓮が、外国の侵略のような国家的危機が発生すると鎌倉幕府に警告してからすぐ、実際にモンゴルが日本に軍隊を派遣してきた。この後日蓮は、予言者としても広く知られるようになった。日蓮はあまりにも熱を入れて活動したため、幕府から何度か刑を科せられた。

　これらの新しい宗派は、中世ヨーロッパのローマカトリック教会への反対者になぞらえることができる。なぜなら彼らは伝統的な仏教について、その莫大な富、官僚的なやり方、腐敗行為、政治的影響力を槍玉に挙げて批判したからである。そ

日蓮(1222–1282)。鎌倉時代の僧侶

Nichiren (1222–1282), a Buddhist monk in Kamakura Period

9. Creation of People's Buddhism

During the Kamakura Period (1185–1333), many new Buddhist sects were established. Among the most important was Jodo-shu, or the Pure Land Sect. Jodo-shu originated in the tenth century as Jodo-kyo, became known as Jodo-shu under the priest Honen, and was further developed by the priest Shinran as Jodo Shinshu, or the New Pure Land Sect, in 1224.

The central tenet of Jodo Shinshu held that if people repeat the *nembutsu* chant ("I take refuge in Amida Buddha"), they will be saved after death because of the boundless mercy of Amida (Amitābha). In addition, Jodo Shinshu believed that this world is like an illusion, that nobody or nothing lasts forever, so just to believe and to utter the *nembutsu* meant salvation after death. Jodo Shinshu was quite popular because of its simple philosophy. It also responded to the needs of the era, when society was unstable because of war, disease, and poverty.

Nichiren-shu, another sect established in the thirteenth century, by the priest Nichiren, centered on recitation of the Hoke-kyo, or Lotus Sutra, a key Buddhist text. Nichiren was an exclusivist and criticized other religious sects that did not follow his beliefs and practices. After he warned Kamakura that there would be a national crisis, such as a foreign invasion, and Mongolia did in fact send troops to Japan soon thereafter, he also became widely known as a prophet. His activities were so zealous that he was prosecuted several times by the shogunate.

These new sects can be compared to dissenters against the Roman Catholic Church in medieval Europe, because they criticized traditional Buddhism for its great wealth, bureaucratic ways, corruption, and political influence. While traditional Buddhism and the shogunate saw these sects as threats, vast numbers of ordinary people accepted them as more

第3章 中世社会

れまでの仏教と幕府はこれらの新しい宗派を脅威とみなしたが、一方で、膨大な数の民衆が新しい宗派を受け入れた。厳しい研鑽と修行を必要とする既存の仏教よりも、親しみやすく分かりやすかったからである。結果的に、これらの新しい宗派は、間もなく日本の仏教における主流となった。

　13世紀には、もう一つの重要な宗派である禅宗が中国の宋朝から日本に伝えられた。禅宗は、日常生活で遭遇する問題を克服するため、瞑想の修行と身体の鍛錬を重んじる。その禁欲的な考え方から、禅宗は、心身の厳しい鍛錬を重視する武士階級の間で広まった。多くの禅寺（特に鎌倉と京都に非常に多い）が12世紀から15世紀の間に建立され、有力な武士の支援を受けた。それらの禅寺は、建築様式、彫刻、塗装だけでなく、庭園もまた美観に優れていた。庭園は、瞑想の環境としてとりわけ重要な役割を果たした。京都の南禅寺、龍安寺、大徳寺は、そのような美しい庭園を特徴とする、最も重要な禅寺である。鎌倉には、建長寺や円覚寺などがある。

　現在でも、浄土宗、日蓮宗、禅宗は、日本の三大仏教宗派である。

建長寺の正門（山門）。12世紀における禅寺の典型的な形式である

The main gate of Kencho-ji temple is in the typical style of the Zen temples of the twelfth century

intimate and easier to understand than established Buddhism, which required rigorous study and training. As a result, these new sects soon entered the mainstream of Japanese Buddhism.

Another important sect, Zen, was introduced to Japan from the Song Dynasty in China in the thirteenth century. Zen values the disciplines of meditation and physical training to overcome the troubles of daily life. Because of its stoic way of thought, Zen was widespread among the samurai class, which emphasized strict mental and physical discipline. Many Zen temples, which are particularly numerous in Kamakura and Kyoto, were built between the twelfth and fifteenth centuries and were supported by powerful warriors. They were not only beautiful for their architecture, sculpture, and painting, but also for their gardens. Gardens played a particularly important role as settings for meditation. Nanzen-ji, Ryoan-ji, and Daitoku-ji in Kyoto are the most important Zen temples featuring such beautiful gardens. In Kamakura, there are Kencho-ji and Engaku-ji, among others.

Even now Jodo-shu, Nichiren-shu and Zen are the three largest Buddhist sects in Japan.

世界的に有名な龍安寺石庭。
15世紀末期に作庭された

The internationally-known rock garden at Ryoan-ji temple was created in the late fifteenth century

10. 元寇と鎌倉幕府の崩壊

　日本でこれらの新しい宗派が急激に広まっていった時期、中国は北方からの大規模な侵攻を受けていた。初めに満州人が華北に侵攻し、その後南宋を打倒した。二度目の侵攻の波はモンゴルから押し寄せ、満州人の領土を奪い、華北に新しい帝国、元朝を建国した。

　モンゴル帝国は、中東やヨーロッパにまで及ぶ大帝国であった。元朝の統合後、元の皇帝の中で最有力者であったフビライ・ハンは、日本へと目を向けた。1274年の初回侵攻時、フビライ・ハンは、火薬を用いた先進兵器を携えた、高麗とモンゴルから成る３万の軍勢を派遣した。しかしながら、台風により連合軍の船は撤退を余儀なくされ、計画は失敗に終わった。その後、元は南宋を征服し、中国全土を支配下に置いた。

　1281年に再度、フビライ・ハンは、高麗、モンゴル、中国勢15万の軍を高麗と中国南部から派遣して侵攻した。これは、第二次世界大戦後に日本が連合国に占領された1945年よりも前に、日本国土が受けた唯一の侵攻であった。

モンゴル人と日本の武士との戦い
Fighting between Mongolians and a Japanese warrior

10. Mongolian Invasion and the Fall of Kamakura

During the time when these new Buddhist sects were proliferating in Japan, China was experiencing a massive invasion from the north. First, the Manchurians invaded northern China and then toppled the Song Dynasty in the south. A second wave of invasions came from Mongolia, usurping Manchurian territory and establishing a new empire, the Yuan Dynasty, in northern China.

The Mongolian empire was vast, extending to the Middle East and even into Europe. After consolidating the Yuan Dynasty, Kublai Khan, the most powerful of the Yuan emperors, turned his eyes toward Japan. In his first attempt in 1274, he sent 30,000 Korean and Mongolian troops with advanced weapons using gunpowder. However, a typhoon forced their ships back and foiled their plans. Thereafter, the Yuan vanquished the Southern Song Dynasty and subjugated all of China.

Kublai Khan made another attempt in 1281 with 150,000 Korean, Mongolian, and Chinese soldiers, dispatched from Korea and southern China. This was the only invasion of Japanese soil prior to 1945, when Japan was occupied by the Allied nations after World War II.

フビライ・ハン。13世紀に自らの支配下で中国を統一した、初のモンゴル人皇帝

Kublai Khan, the first Mongolian emperor, united China under his rule in the thirteenth century

日本人は、どのようにして自らを防御したのであろうか。まず、彼らは備えが十分であった。一度目の侵攻後、日本人は、北九州の博多湾岸に防塁を築いた。これによって侵攻軍は、54日間湾岸で足止めされることとなった。次にモンゴル軍は海戦に不慣れであり、小型船に乗った日本軍の攻撃に苦戦した。そしてさらに、突然また新たな台風が発生し、今度はモンゴル軍を打ち破ることとなった。

二度にわたりタイミングよく台風に救われたため、人々はこの出来事を、神道の神と、自然と自然の力を崇拝するその教義がもたらした奇跡とみなすようになった。この二つの台風は神風と称された。この考えは、日本人が神に守られている民族であるという日本人独自の思想をもたらした。そして後に、第二次世界大戦に至る数年の間、軍国主義のプロパガンダでこの思想が利用されることとなった。

二度の失敗の後、モンゴルはもう侵攻を試みることはなかった。しかしながら、失敗に終わった侵攻は、ヨーロッパにおいて注目すべき結果をもたらした。イタリアの商人マルコ・ポーロは、この時期元朝に仕えており、日本を黄金の国として西洋に紹介した。この結果、アジアへのヨーロッパ人渡来が促進された。元寇は鎌倉幕府にも経済的な損害を与え、社会不安を引き起こした。その後、幕府内の経済問題や政治問題を解決できる有能な指導者が現れることはなかった。

最終的に、幕府内の有力な支持者は去っていき、鎌倉幕府に対抗するため朝廷の一員となった。社会的混乱が数年続いた後、幕府における最も有力な二つの氏族、新田氏と足利氏は鎌倉幕府を裏切る決意をした。その結果、幕府を支持し実権を握っていた北条氏は滅亡し、1333年にその政権は終わりを迎えることとなった。同時に、京都の朝廷は、後醍醐天皇の指揮下で新政権を樹立した。

How did the Japanese defend themselves? First, they were well prepared. After the first invasion attempt, they erected walls around Hakata Bay in northern Kyushu, which kept the invaders immobilized for fifty-four days on the seashore. Second, the Mongols were not used to fighting at sea and were harried by Japanese attacking in small boats. And third, yet another typhoon suddenly arose, this time destroying the Mongolian fleet.

Having been twice saved by timely typhoons, people looked upon them as miracles vouchsafed by the gods of Shinto and its doctrine of reverence for nature and nature's power. They referred to these two typhoons as *kamikaze*, or divine winds. This belief contributed to the Japanese notion of their own uniqueness—that is, that the Japanese were a divinely favored people—and was later used in militaristic propaganda in the years leading up to World War II.

After failing twice, the Mongols did not try again. However, the attempted invasions brought one noteworthy result in Europe. The Italian merchant Marco Polo, who served the Yuan Dynasty around this time, introduced Japan to the West as a land overflowing with gold and thus stimulated Europeans to travel to Asia. The Mongolian invasions also damaged the Kamakura shogunate economically and caused social unrest. Subsequently, no talented leaders arose who could resolve the economic and political problems inside the shogunate.

Finally, powerful supporters inside the shogunate decamped and joined the imperial court to oppose Kamakura. After several years of turbulence, the Nitta and Ashikaga, the two most powerful shogunate clans, decided to betray Kamakura. Thus, the Hojo clan, the actual power behind the shogunate, perished, and its government came to an end in 1333. Simultaneously, the imperial court in Kyoto established a new government under the leadership of Emperor Godaigo.

11. 南北朝時代

　鎌倉幕府が崩壊した時、天皇は、古代日本のような朝廷の権威を再び確立しようとしていた。しかしながら、建武の新政として知られるこの試みはすぐに破綻した。なぜなら、14世紀の武家社会における現実とは相容れなかったからである。武士の支持を受けた足利氏はついに京都の新政権を崩壊させ、分家から成るもう一つの朝廷を作った。その間、後醍醐天皇は奈良県南部の吉野へ逃れて、1336年にいわゆる南朝を樹立した。

　一方で京都の朝廷は、足利氏の当主である足利尊氏を新しい征夷大将軍に任命した。このようにして足利幕府が京都に成立し、その所在地にちなんで室町幕府と呼ばれることとなった。

　二つの朝廷に二人の天皇が存在したこの時代は、中国の歴史における同様の時代にちなんで、南北朝時代と呼ばれている。初めの30年間は、足利幕府に多くの厳しい難題を

後醍醐天皇
Emperor Godaigo

足利尊氏。室町（足利）幕府の初代将軍
Ashikaga Takauji, the first shogun of the Muromachi (Ashikaga) shogunate

11. Era of Two Imperial Courts

When the Kamakura shogunate fell, the emperor's intent was to re-establish the authority of the imperial court as in ancient Japan. However, this attempt, known as the Kemmu Restoration, quickly failed, as it was incompatible with the reality of samurai society in the fourteenth century. The Ashikaga clan, supported by the samurai, finally wiped out the new government in Kyoto and created another imperial court with a branch family. Meanwhile, Emperor Godaigo escaped to Yoshino, south of Nara, and set up the so-called Southern Court in 1336.

At the same time, the imperial court in Kyoto appointed Ashikaga Takauji, head of the Ashikaga clan, as the new shogun. Thus, the Ashikaga shogunate was established in Kyoto and referred to as the Muromachi shogunate, named after the place where it was located.

This period of two imperial courts, with two emperors, is called the Southern and Northern Courts era, named after a similar period in Chinese history. The first thirty years presented a number of critical

楠木正成像。南朝の有力な支持者

Statue of Kusunoki Masashige, powerful supporter of the Southern Court

突き付けた。恐らく最も大きな難題は、かつて足利尊氏の支持者だったが、忠誠の対象を南朝に変更した山名氏によってもたらされた。山名氏側を率いる北畠親房は、後醍醐を正統な天皇として再び擁立することに、とりわけ熱心であった。北畠親房の優れた戦略とゲリラ戦術は、足利幕府からも大きく注目されることとなった。一方、尊氏とその弟との争いが内部抗争を誘発して、北朝の存在理由をさらに弱めることとなった。

　繰り返し続いた騒動や混乱も、第三代足利将軍義満の頃にようやく制圧された。義満は、1368年にわずか11歳で征夷大将軍に任命された。やがて、主要な武家を統率する上で義満は巧みな政治手腕を発揮するようになり、ついには強固な専制権力を確立するまでになった。

　1392年、南北朝それぞれの家系から交互に皇位継承するよう求める和約に合意することで、義満は南朝を説得して京都に帰還させた。さらには天皇を説得して、朝廷における最高位を自身に与えさせた。後に義満は自らの約束を破って後醍醐一族をないがしろにし、同一族から天皇に即位する者は出なかった。だが義満の権力はすでに確立しており、足利氏は卓越した氏族となっていた。

足利義満
Ashikaga Yoshimitsu

challenges to the Ashikaga shogunate. Perhaps the biggest challenge came from the Yamana clan, a former ally of Ashikaga Takauji, which changed its allegiance to the Southern Court. One Yamana leader, Kitabatake Chikafusa, was particularly zealous in the cause of re-establishing Godaigo as the legitimate emperor. His excellent strategy and guerrilla tactics occupied much of the Ashikaga shogunate's attention. Meanwhile, a quarrel between Takauji and his brother fomented internal conflict, further weakening the cause of the Northern Court.

The continual tumult and turmoil was finally brought under control around the time of the third Ashikaga shogun, Yoshimitsu. He had been appointed shogun in 1368 when he was only eleven years old. Over time, he demonstrated a deft political talent at managing the major samurai clans, eventually establishing an iron-clad dictatorship.

Yoshimitsu persuaded the Southern Court to return to Kyoto in 1392 by agreeing to a compromise calling for imperial succession to alternate between the lines of the Southern and Northern Courts. He also persuaded the emperor to confer on him the highest rank at the imperial court. Later he reneged on his promise, ignoring the Godaigo line (it supplied no further emperors), but his power had been consolidated and the Ashikaga clan was preeminent.

12. 繁栄から混沌へ

　自らの政治権力を確固たるものにした義満は、京都と鎌倉における新たな禅寺の熱心な支援者となった。京都では、南禅寺、大徳寺、天龍寺、妙心寺、東福寺など、大規模な禅寺の建立を次々に支援した。また、鹿苑寺の敷地内に自らの有名な別荘である金閣寺も建立した。金箔で覆われたこの別荘は今日、京都において最も人気がある観光名所の一つとなっている。この時代は壮麗な仏教文化の最高潮を示しており、その文化は義満の別荘が京都の北部にある山の麓に位置することから、北山と呼ばれた。

　15世紀の終わりが近づくにつれて、足利幕府は衰退していった。その要因の一つは、激化する幕府内の権力争いであり、これをきっかけに、有力な氏族が国の統治において自己主張をするようになった。もう一つの要因は、元々足利幕府に支援されていた寺院が、自らの影響力を行使し始めたことである。

　室町（足利）時代には、元来は鎌倉幕府から国司に任命された地方の武家が、各自の地域で政治勢力を拡大した。足利幕府は、それらの武家を一致団結させて統制する権力の

東福寺
Tofuku-ji temple

足利義政
Ashikaga Yoshimasa

Chapter 3: Medieval Society

12. From Prosperity to Chaos

After his political power was consolidated, Yoshimitsu became an avid supporter of new Zen temples in Kyoto and Kamakura. In Kyoto, he backed the construction of a series of large Zen temples, including Nanzen-ji, Daitoku-ji, Tenryu-ji, Myoshin-ji, and Tofuku-ji. He also constructed his famous villa, Kinkaku-ji, or the Temple of the Golden Pavilion, inside the Rokuon-ji temple grounds. Today this gold-foiled villa is one of the most popular tourist attractions in Kyoto. This era marked the height of a magnificent Buddhist culture, called Kitayama, or Northern Mountain, because Yoshimitsu's villa was located at the foot of the mountains north of Kyoto.

Toward the end of the fifteenth century, the Ashikaga shogunate fell into decline. One factor was the escalating internal power struggles, giving powerful clans a chance to assert themselves in governing the nation. Another was that, temples originally supported by the Ashikaga shogunate started to exercise their influence.

During the Muromachi (Ashikaga) era, local samurai clans, which were originally appointed as provincial governors by the Kamakura shogunate, extended their political power in their respective areas. The

天龍寺
Tenryu-ji temple

南禅寺
Nanzen-ji temple

55

中枢となるはずであった。しかしながら、足利幕府内の争いによって、在地の武家領主は独立する機会を得ることとなった。応仁の乱(1467–77)の勃発により、足利幕府は致命的な損害を受けた。戦闘の多くは京都で行われ、京都は修復不可能なほどの損害を被った。

このような争いの最中に、第八代足利将軍の義政は京都の東山に隠居し、そこに銀閣寺と呼ばれる別荘を建てた。彼は、政治や争いにうんざりしていたため、その別荘で芸術や演劇に没頭した。義政の保護下で、観阿弥とその息子の世阿弥によって、能楽（舞踊、音楽、歌を組み合わせた仮面劇）が発展したのがこの時期である。

能舞台
Noh theater

実際に、京都の寺院の多くが、市内北部および東部の山や丘に現存する。応仁の乱による被害から比較的安全なのがそれらの地域であったためである。応仁の乱の間に、将軍は武士階級の象徴に過ぎないとみなされるようになった。一方、地方では、在地領主が自らの影響力と領土を拡大するために同士討ちをした。これが戦国時代の始まりである。

13. 戦国時代

15世紀後半に、足利幕府は政治的な力を失った。それから間もなく、主要な在地領主が、独自の法制度や政治体制を構築した。彼らはまるで独立した国家のように振る舞い、その支配下にある農村部は繁栄し始めた。主要都市の市場

Ashikaga shogunate was meant to be the power center that united and controlled those clans. Ashikaga's internal conflicts, however, provided an opportunity for local clan lords to become independent. When the Onin War (1467–77) broke out, it inflicted fatal damage on the Ashikaga. Much of the fighting took place in Kyoto, and the city suffered irreparably.

During these struggles, Ashikaga Yoshimasa, the eighth Ashikaga shogun, retired to the eastern mountains of Kyoto, where he created the villa called Ginkaku-ji, or the Temple of the Silver Pavilion. In his villa he devoted himself to art and theater, having grown tired of politics and fighting. It was at this time, under Yoshimasa's patronage, that the Noh theater (masked drama combining dance, music, and chant) was developed by Kan'ami and his son Zeami.

In fact, many of Kyoto's temples are now located in the mountains and hills north and east of the city, as those areas were relatively safe from the ravages of the Onin War. During that war, the shogun came to be regarded as nothing more than a symbol of samurai hierarchy, while in the provinces local lords fought among themselves to expand their influence and territory. This marked the beginning of the Warring States Period.

13. The Warring States Period

Soon after the Ashikaga shogunate became politically ineffective in the late fifteenth century, major local lords created their own legal and political systems. They acted as though they were independent countries, and rural areas under their control began to flourish. In their major cities

は、制限を受けず自由に発展していた。京都の洗練された文化や、また外国文化も、地方にまで浸透していた。

　この時期は、多様性とチャンスの時代であった。中央の指導力が弱まったことで中世の体制が脆弱になったため、古い階級制度そのものが徐々に変化した。この傾向は、在地領主による政治においても見られた。下級武士が名目上の領主から権力を奪って自らを領主そのものだと称することも、比較的よく起きるようになった。地方分権化がさらに進むにつれて、日本全国の経済活動や文化活動は、新たに生まれ変わった。

　また、この地方分権化により、地方都市や城下町が急増した。このような新しい町の一つに、大阪のすぐ南に位置する堺がある。急成長を遂げた堺は、やがて「自由都市」の様相を呈するようになった。堺は、交易の中心地として十分に重要な地位と権力を手に入れて幕府と企業体として取引できるまでになり、独自の法律を施行する自由も獲得した。一時期など、幕府が堺の商人からの借金に頼ったことすらあった。

　この時代、堺や近隣の兵庫（現在の神戸）を中心として、中国との貿易が大幅に増加した。中国からの輸入品で最も重要だったものの一つが銅銭であった。この頃の日本は自国の硬貨を鋳造しておらず、貿易の拡大において、通貨は中国の硬貨に頼っていた。この時代の輸入品には、鉄、織物、薬品、書物、美術品などがあった。中国との貿易は非常に有益であった。なぜなら、日本製品は中国市場で本国の5

中国に向かう日本の貿易船
China-bound Japanese trading ship

Chapter 3: Medieval Society

the markets were unrestricted and grew freely. Kyoto's sophisticated culture, and foreign culture as well, filtered down to the local level.

It was a time of diversity and opportunity. As the medieval system declined due to weakened central leadership, the old hierarchical system itself gradually changed. This trend can be seen in the politics of local lords. It became relatively common for lower-ranking samurai to usurp power from their nominal lords and set themselves up as lords themselves. With greater decentralization, economic and cultural activity throughout Japan took on new life.

This decentralization also resulted in the proliferation of provincial and castle towns. One of these new towns, called Sakai, located just south of Osaka, underwent rapid growth and eventually took on the guise of a "free city." It gained enough importance and power as a trading center that it was able to bargain as a corporate entity with the shogunate. Sakai also gained some freedom to administer its own laws, and at one time the shogunate even resorted to borrowing money from the city's merchants.

Trade with China increased greatly during this period, being centered in Sakai and nearby Hyogo, currently Kobe. One of the most important imports from China was copper money. Japan was not at this time minting its own coins, so expanding trade relied on Chinese coins for currency. Iron, textiles, drugs, books, and art were among the goods imported during this period. The trade

永楽通宝と呼ばれた硬貨。中国の明朝で鋳造され、日本で通貨として使用された

This coin, called an Eiraku Tsuho, was minted in Ming Dynasty China and used as currency in Japan

59

倍から10倍の価格で販売されたからである。人気の高い輸出品の中には、刀などの武器、漆器や扇子などの高級品が挙げられる。

多くの激戦が繰り広げられた16世紀前半には、有力な新しい領主の中で、自分よりはるかに強大な権力者と手を組む者もいた。この時代に最も活躍した戦国大名に、南九州の島津氏、中国地方の毛利氏、本州中部の武田氏、北陸の上杉氏、関東の北条氏、東北の伊達氏がいた。

武田信玄
Takeda Shingen

上杉謙信
Uesugi Kenshin

伊達政宗
Date Masamune

14. 西洋文化の到来

この時代を最も豊かにした特徴の一つに、国際交流があった。16世紀のヨーロッパにおける宗教改革によって、ヨーロッパ諸国間では対立や争いが引き起こされた。さらにトルコのオスマン帝国がヨーロッパに影響力を拡大しており、ヨーロッパ列強は、東洋と西洋との間で経済交流や文化交流が制限されていると感じていた。その結果、ポルトガル、スペイン、イタリアといったカトリックの国々は、自らの宗教的影響力をヨーロッパ以外にも拡大することを目指し、東洋への航路を開拓した。中国はこの時代、1368年頃から

with China was immensely profitable, since Japanese goods sold in the Chinese market for five to ten times their value at home. Popular exports included weapons such as swords and luxury items like lacquerware and fans.

During the first half of the sixteenth century, there were many hard-fought battles, and some powerful new lords aligned with much bigger powers. Among the most active warlords of this period were the lord of Shimazu in southern Kyushu, the lord of Mori in the Chugoku region, the lord of Takeda in central Honshu, the lord of Uesugi in Hokuriku, the lord of Hojo in Kanto, and the lord of Date in Tohoku.

14. The Advent of Western Culture

One of the most enriching aspects of this period was global exchange. The Protestant Reformation in sixteenth-century Europe fomented conflict and competition among European countries. In addition, the Ottoman Empire in Turkey expanded its influence into Europe, and European powers felt restraints on economic and cultural exchange between East and West. As a result, Catholic nations such as Portugal, Spain, and Italy, hoping to expand their religious influence beyond Europe, explored ocean routes to the East. China at this time had been united under the Ming Dynasty since around 1368. Ashikaga

明朝の支配下で統一されていた。足利義満は、1404年に明と公式の貿易関係を開始した。

公式の貿易だけでなく、違法貿易もあった。中国では、倭寇と呼ばれる日本の海賊が中国の海岸線における略奪で悪名を馳せていた。さらに、日本の西部と南部における多くの在地領主、豪商、いくつかの大寺院が、高麗と中国に個人として貿易使節団を派遣した。明朝の繁栄もまたヨーロッパ人を魅了し、彼らの多くが中国南部に移り住んだ。アジアへの航路が発見されてからは、特にこの傾向が顕著であった。アジアにいたヨーロッパ人の中で、最も人数が多く影響力が強かったのは、ポルトガル人であった。彼らは1543年に日本の南九州沖にある種子島に上陸し、鉄砲とその関連技術を持ち込んだ。

1549年、日本にキリスト教を伝えたのもポルトガル人である。イエズス会の宣教師、フランシスコ・ザビエルが、他のアジア諸国で伝道した後、日本に到着した際のことである。この新たな宗教を歓迎する大名も多く、誠実な信者になる者もいた。一方、キリスト教徒がもたらした貿易や技術的利点に対して関心を向ける大名も存在した。イエズ

フランシスコ・ザビエル（1506–62）。イエズス会の創設者の一人。日本にキリスト教を伝えた

Francisco Xavier (1506–62), a co-founder of the Society of Jesus, brought Christianity to Japan

Yoshimitsu opened official trade relationships with the Ming in 1404.

In addition to official trade, there was also illegal trade. Japanese pirates, called Wokou (Wako in Japanese), were well-known in China from their plundering of its coastline. Moreover, many local lords in western and southern Japan, wealthy merchants, and some large temples sent private trade missions to Korea and China. The Ming Dynasty's prosperity also attracted Europeans and many of them settled in southern China. This was especially true after the discovery of an ocean route to Asia. Among the most numerous and influential of the Europeans in Asia were the Portuguese, who landed on the Japanese island of Tanegashima off southern Kyushu in 1543. They brought with them firearms and related technology.

In 1549 the Portuguese also introduced Christianity when the Jesuit priest Francis Xavier arrived after preaching in other Asian countries. Many Japanese lords welcomed the new religion, some becoming sincere believers, while others were more interested in the trade and technological advantages that Christianity offered. The Jesuit Alessandro

細部
Detail

来日外国人を描いた屏風
Folding screen depicting foreigners in Japan

ス会のアレッサンドロ・ヴァリニャーノは1582年、日本には15万人の改宗キリスト教徒がいて200の教会があるとローマに報告した。同じ年、名門の出身である日本人キリスト教徒で構成された使節団が、ローマ教皇とスペイン国王を訪問するために派遣された。

イエズス会の宣教師たちは特に京都で成功を収め、多くの有力大名との関係を構築した。京都における仏教の権威者たちはキリスト教徒の成功に不安を抱き、彼らを追放するよう幕府に圧力をかけた。宣教師たちは堺に逃れたが、堺の商人への伝道は、それほど上手くはいかなかった。

15. 再統一

西洋文化とのこのような出合いは、そこここで戦闘が繰り広げられていたこの国が統一へと向かっている時に生じた。1550年頃日本はまだ分裂しており、主要な戦国大名が徐々に領土を拡大し、弱小領地の管轄区域を吸収していた。一連の戦いの後、尾張（現在の愛知県西部）の大名であった織田信長は1573年、足利幕府を打倒するため京都に軍隊を送り込んだ。これに成功した信長は、第十五代足利将軍義昭を京都から追放した。信長は義昭の後継者を選定しなかったため、室町幕府と足利家はこれで終わりを迎えることとなった。信長自身も将軍の称号を手に入れることはせず、軍事的覇権を維持しつつ皇統を支えることを選んだ。

信長は、日本の歴史上最も人気の高い人物の一人である。彼は小大名の息子だったが、急速に領土を拡大した。軍事

織田信長
Oda Nobunaga

Valignano reported to Rome in 1582 that there were 150,000 Christian converts and two hundred churches in Japan. In the same year, a delegation of Japanese Christians of noble lineage was sent to visit the Pope and the king of Spain.

The Jesuit priests were particularly successful in Kyoto, forging relationships with many influential lords. The Buddhist authorities there, alarmed at Christianity's success, brought pressure on the government to have these priests expelled. These priests retreated to Sakai, but their message was not as successful with the city's merchant population.

15. Reunification

This encounter with Western culture took place at a time when the embattled country was moving toward unification. Around 1550, the country was still divided, with the major warlords having gradually expanded their territory and absorbed the jurisdictions of weaker domains. In 1573, after a series of battles, Oda Nobunaga, the lord of Owari (currently western Aichi Prefecture), sent his armies into Kyoto to topple the Ashikaga shogunate. Nobunaga succeeded and expelled Ashikaga Yoshiaki, the fifteenth Ashikaga shogun, from the capital. This ended the Muromachi shogunate and the Ashikaga line, as Nobunaga did not choose a successor for Yoshiaki. Neither did Nobunaga take the title of shogun for himself, preferring to support the imperial line while maintaining military hegemony.

Nobunaga is one of the most popular figures in Japanese history.

戦略の天才で、闘争的な指導者であった。西洋の影響を歓迎し、自らの領土を豊かにするためにそれを活用した。鉄砲の威力を高く評価し、1575年、盟友の徳川家康とともに強敵の武田氏を打ち破った（長篠の戦い）際には、鉄砲を効果的に使用した。

信長はその後、本拠地を京都に近い琵琶湖岸の安土に移し、再統一事業に着手した。安土にはヨーロッパの宣教師も住んでおり、国際的な雰囲気が漂っていた。安土城は、その壮麗さからローマでも知られていた。信長は天下統一のため、宗教問題だけでなく政治的な問題にも影響力を持っている、仏教の権威者との対立も辞さなかった。

明智光秀。織田信長を裏切り殺害した武将

Akechi Mitsuhide, the general who betrayed and killed Oda Nobunaga

信長は次に、地方の支配に着手した。しかし、信長の軍勢の大半が、本州西部の有力者である毛利氏を攻撃している間に、信長は自らが率いる武将の一人、明智光秀の裏切りにあった。1582年、京都を通過中だった信長は、本能寺で明智の奇襲を受けた。捕らわれまいと自害をした信長の体は、燃えゆく寺院の炎に包まれた。

長篠の戦いを描いた屏風

Folding screen depicting Battle of Nagashino

He was the son of a minor lord but expanded his territory rapidly. He was a genius at military strategy and an aggressive leader. He welcomed Western influence and used it to enrich his territory. He valued the power of firearms and used them effectively when he and his ally, Tokugawa Ieyasu, defeated the Takeda clan, a powerful rival, in 1575.

Nobunaga then relocated his headquarters to Azuchi, on the shore of Lake Biwa near Kyoto, and started the process of reunification. Azuchi had an international atmosphere, with several European missionaries residing there. The Azuchi Castle was known even in Rome for its magnificence. To reunify the country, Nobunaga didn't hesitate to clash with Buddhist authorities, who were influential not only in religious affairs but in political matters as well.

Next Nobunaga began the process of subjugating the outlying regions. However, while the majority of his troops were engaged in assailing the powerful Mori of western Honshu, he was betrayed by one of his own generals, Akechi Mitsuhide. While Nobunaga was passing through Kyoto in 1582, Akechi took him by surprise in a temple called Honno-ji. To avoid capture, Nobunaga committed suicide, his body consumed in the flames of the burning temple.

安土城。1582年の織田信長の死後すぐに廃城となった

Azuchi Castle, destroyed immediately after the death of Oda Nobunaga in 1582

16. 豊臣秀吉とその時代

　信長の夢であった天下統一を実現した武将は、豊臣秀吉であった。信長のおかげで、秀吉は、最下層の武士階級から信長の最高武将の一人にまで昇進した。信長が死去した時、秀吉は毛利氏に対する攻撃を主導していた。信長の死を知らされた秀吉は、すぐに毛利氏と講和を結び、信長の死の仇討ちをするため急いで京都に戻って明智を討った。その後、秀吉はさらに他の敵を打ち負かし、1590年、北条氏の滅亡によって自らの（そして信長の）夢を実現した。

　豊臣秀吉の政権はそれまでの武家政権とは異なり、秀吉は単に最高位の大名とみなされた。つまり秀吉の権力は、地方で任命された国司（それぞれが独自の管轄と軍事制度を持つ）に支えられた中央集権国家に由来するものではない。秀吉は優れた武将として、また日本の最有力者として国司の尊敬を得た。

　そうした立場から秀吉は度量衡の改定、検地の実施、新税制の設定を実施した。また、身分の階層化を厳しく実施し、武士以外の者が武器を所有することを禁じた。秀吉は本拠地を大坂に設置し、そこに大坂城を築いた。また京都にも豪華な別荘を所有し、当地から寺院や朝廷を統制した。

豊臣秀吉。100年に及ぶ内乱の後、日本を統一した独裁者
Toyotomi Hideyoshi, the dictator who united Japan after 100 years of civil war

大坂城。1583年に豊臣秀吉が最初に築いた
Osaka Castle, originally erected by Toyotomi Hideyoshi in 1583

16. Toyotomi Hideyoshi and His Era

The general who fulfilled Nobunaga's dream of uniting the country was Toyotomi Hideyoshi. He had been promoted by Nobunaga from the lowest samurai rank to become one of his top generals. At the time of Nobunaga's death, Hideyoshi was leading the assault against the Mori. Receiving word of Nobunaga's death, he quickly concluded a peace treaty with the Mori and rushed back to Kyoto to avenge Nobunaga's death by squelching Akechi. He then proceeded to bring down his remaining rivals, and in 1590 his (and Nobunaga's) dream was realized with the fall of the Hojo.

Toyotomi Hideyoshi's government was different from the former military governments in that he was considered simply as the highest-ranking lord. In other words, his authority did not come from a centralized government supported by locally appointed governors, each with his own jurisdiction and military system. He won their respect as a brilliant general and as the most powerful person in the land.

In that capacity, Hideyoshi reformed the system of weights and measures, conducted land surveys, and created a new tax system. Also, he strictly enforced class stratification and prohibited non-samurai from possessing weapons. His headquarters was established in Osaka, where

聚楽第。豊臣秀吉が、政庁兼邸宅として使用した豪華な屋敷
Jurakudai. This gorgeous palace was used by Toyotomi Hideyoshi for both official business and as a private residence

第3章 中世社会

信長と秀吉の時代を安土桃山時代と呼ぶ。特定の芸術形式が最高の表現に到達した時代である。多くの絵画が、城、寺院、別荘の壁や襖に描かれた。その中に、当時最も影響力が強い画家集団であった狩野派の作品もあった。茶道を洗練した形としたのは、千利休（秀吉のもとに仕えた有名な商人であり茶人）であった。

千利休。16世紀に活躍した茶人。豊臣秀吉の側近として仕えた

Sen no Rikyu, tea ceremony master active in the sixteenth century. He served as an advisor to Toyotomi Hideyoshi

絵画や茶道は、貴族階級や武家の生活様式に溶け込んだ。一方で、多くの商人や芸術家が魅惑的な西洋文化を称賛した。自由な国際貿易の町として知られる堺の町は、信長が政権に就くまで、商人自らが運営に当たっていた。殺戮の戦国時代、有力な在地領主からの投資によって日本の経済や生活様式が繁栄したのは皮肉なことである。信長と秀吉もまた、領土を拡大していた時にそのような投資の利益を受け継ぎ、強力な財政基盤を築くことができたのである。

しかし秀吉の政治経歴は、上手くいったことばかりではなかった。秀吉は、中国の明朝を征服する狙いを持って、二度朝鮮への侵攻を試みた。初回は1592年、15万人の兵士を朝鮮半島に派遣した。日本軍はソウルと平壌を占領したが、中国軍と朝鮮水軍が支援したゲリラ型の反撃を受け、撤退を余儀なくされた。二度目の攻撃は、1598年の秀吉の死によって中止された。失敗に終わったこれらの侵攻は、1910年の日本による韓国併合と関連して言及されることがある。

he built Osaka Castle. He also had luxurious villas in Kyoto, from which he exercised control over the temples and imperial court.

The era of Nobunaga and Hideyoshi is called Azuchi-Momoyama, a period when certain art forms achieved their highest expression. Many paintings were created on the walls and sliding doors of castles, temples, and villas, including works by the Kano school of painters, the most influential of the time. The tea ceremony was refined by Sen no Rikyu, the famous merchant and tea master serving under Hideyoshi.

Painting and the tea ceremony were integrated into the lifestyles of the noble and military classes. Many merchants and artists, on the other hand, appreciated exotic Western culture. The city of Sakai, known as a free international trading city, was governed by the merchants themselves until Nobunaga came to power. Ironically, during the internecine Warring States Period, the Japanese economy and lifestyle flourished, thanks to the investment of powerful local lords. When Nobunaga and Hideyoshi expanded their territory, they also inherited the benefits of those investments and were able to create a strong financial foundation.

But Hideyoshi's political career was not always successful. He tried twice to invade Korea, with an eye to conquering the Chinese Ming Dynasty. His first attempt was in 1592, when he dispatched 150,000 soldiers to the Korean Peninsula. Although they captured Seoul and Pyongyang, they were forced to withdraw by a guerrilla-style counterattack supported by Chinese troops and the Korean navy. Hideyoshi's second attempt was aborted due to his death in 1598. These failed incursions are sometimes mentioned in connection with the Japanese annexation of Korea in 1910.

第4章 将軍と鎖国

17. 徳川幕府の創設

　秀吉が死の床に就いていた頃、息子の秀頼はまだ小さな子供だった。秀吉は五大老を任命して、秀頼が成人して指導力を発揮するまでの後見役に当たらせた。大老の中で最も影響力が強かったのは、本州中央の関東平野の領主であった徳川家康である。家康は名古屋の東、三河の弱小領主の下に生まれた。織田信長が一人の指導者の下で国家統一に向けて前進を始めると、家康は信長の野望を支持した。

　信長の暗殺後、家康は秀吉に次ぐ権力の座を獲得した。これを認めた秀吉は、1590年に征伐した北条氏が治めていた関東の土地を家康に与えた。その結果、家康を都から遠ざけることになり、秀吉の覇権に対する脅威が減ることになるため、この動きは秀吉にとっては有利であった。しかし、関東はすでに農工業が盛んな地区として発展を遂げており、家康は、自らの権力基盤を拡大させる自由と手段を手にすることとなった。

　家康は秀吉の支配に反対しなかったものの、秀吉が死ぬ頃には多大な影響力を振るい、強い野心も抱いていた。豊臣政権の筆頭家臣であった石田三成は、家康の脅威を感じ取り、積極的に対抗した。

　1600年、両軍は名古屋と京都の中間にある、有名な関ヶ原の戦いでついに激突し、家康軍が三成らの軍勢を破った。

Chapter 4:
Shogun and Seclusion

17. Creation of the Tokugawa Shogunate

When Hideyoshi was on his deathbed, and his son Hideyori was still a small child. Hideyoshi appointed five regents to look after Hideyori until he was old enough to take the reins of leadership. The regent with the strongest influence was Tokugawa Ieyasu, lord of the Kanto plain in central Honshu. He was born in Mikawa, east of Nagoya, the son of a minor lord. When Oda Nobunaga began his push to unite the country under one leader, Ieyasu supported Nobunaga's ambition.

After Nobunaga's assassination, Ieyasu assumed a position of power second only to Hideyoshi. To acknowledge this, Hideyoshi granted Ieyasu the Kanto provinces of the Hojo clan, which he had taken in 1590. This move was beneficial to Hideyoshi because it moved Ieyasu further from the capital, reducing any threat to Hideyoshi's supremacy. However, Kanto was already well developed as an agricultural and industrial region, and it gave Ieyasu the freedom and means to develop his own power base.

Although Ieyasu did not oppose Hideyoshi's leadership, he had become quite influential and ambitious by the time of Hideyoshi's death. Ishida Mitsunari, the top bureaucrat in Hideyoshi's government, sensed the threat posed by Ieyasu and actively opposed him.

The two forces finally clashed in 1600 in the famous Battle of Sekigahara, between Nagoya and Kyoto, with Ieyasu defeating Mitsunari

第4章 将軍と鎖国

　三成の処刑後、家康は江戸（現在の東京）における本拠地を強化した。1603年、天皇は家康を将軍に任命し、1615年に豊臣の最後の砦であった大坂城が落城し、秀吉の息子であった豊臣秀頼が自刃すると、家康の地位は揺るぎないものとなった。

　ジェームズ・クラベルのベストセラー小説「Shōgun」は、17世紀初めのさまざまな出来事に取材している。信長の躍進から1615年の秀頼の死に至るまでの一連の出来事は、多くの日本人作家が小説に取り上げている。また、日本のテレビ局が多くの人気歴史ドラマを制作する際の素材にもなった。

　徳川将軍は1868年まで続き、その後天皇が権力を取り戻して日本は新明治政府の下で近代化を始めることとなる。

大坂城天守閣
Donjon of Osaka Castle

徳川幕府初代将軍・徳川家康
Tokugawa Ieyasu, the first shogun of the Tokugawa shogunate

and his allies. After executing Mitsunari, Ieyasu consolidated his headquarters in Edo (current Tokyo). In 1603, the emperor appointed Ieyasu shogun. His position became unassailable in 1615 with the destruction of Osaka Castle, the last Toyotomi stronghold, which resulted in the suicide of Toyotomi Hideyori, Hideyoshi's son.

Many of the events at the turn of the seventeenth century provided the background for the best-selling novel *Shōgun*, written by James Clavell. This series of incidents, from Nobunaga's rise to the demise of Hideyori in 1615, has been fictionalized by many Japanese novelists. The story also provides material for many a popular historical drama on Japanese television.

The Tokugawa shogunate lasted until 1868, when the emperor was restored to power and Japan started to modernize under the new Meiji government.

石田三成。豊臣秀吉に使えた武将、家老。関ヶ原の戦いの後、徳川家康によって処刑された

Ishida Mitsunari, a general and former senior bureaucrat serving Toyotomi Hideyoshi. He was executed by Tokugawa Ieyasu after the battle of Sekigahara

関ヶ原の戦いの記念碑
Battle of Sekigahara monument

第4章 将軍と鎖国

18. 徳川幕府の基盤形成

　家康とその後継者にとって最も重要な作業は、確固たる政治的基盤を築くことであった。戦国時代の戦いの経験に照らして、徳川家は強力な中央政府を樹立し、全ての大名を監督下に置くこととした。関ヶ原の戦い以前から徳川家に忠誠を誓っていた大名は高い地位に任命され、多くの特権を与えられた。他の大名は僻地へと国替えされ、安全のために権力の座から追われて、問題を起こさないかどうか慎重に監視された。

　家康は、元々漁村に過ぎなかった江戸を徳川将軍の行政的中心地とするべく、巨大な城を建造し、一から都市を築きあげた。家康は、近親者を和歌山（大坂の南）、尾張（名古屋）、水戸（江戸の北）の大名に任命し、これらの要衝の警護に当たらせた。残念ながら、江戸の町（後の東京）や江戸城そのものも、第二次世界大戦中の空襲をはじめとする大火

17世紀の江戸城の絵画
Seventeenth-century painting of Edo Castle

18. The Founding of the Tokugawa Shogunate

The most important task for Ieyasu and his successors was to create a solid political foundation. Based on their experience of civil war during the Warring States Period, they set out to establish a strong centralized government with all local lords under its authority. The lords who had been Tokugawa loyalists before the Battle of Sekigahara were appointed to high offices and granted many privileges. Other lords were relocated to rural areas, safely removed from the seat of power and carefully watched as potential sources of trouble.

Ieyasu built a massive castle and essentially a whole city from scratch in Edo, originally a fishing village, as the administrative center of the Tokugawa shogunate. He appointed his closest relatives as the lords of Wakayama (south of Osaka), Owari (Nagoya) and Mito (north of Edo) to oversee and protect those strategic areas. Unfortunately, the city of Edo (later Tokyo) and the castle itself have been destroyed more than

江戸城 (現皇居) 伏見櫓
Fushimi-yagura keep, Edo Castle (now Imperial Palace)

により一度ならず破壊されている。江戸城が元々あった場所は、現在皇居になっている。

　将軍はまた、京都に行政機関（京都所司代）を置き、朝廷の活動を監視していたが、天皇は理論上神であるとみなされていた。集権政策の一環として、徳川将軍家は日本の利用可能な国土のうち約25％を所有し、残りを大名たちで分けていた。これらの封建領土は藩と呼ばれた。

　社会的安定を生むために、家康は儒教の権威に基づいて階級構造を強化した。家康は国民を4つの階級に分け、最上位を武士とし、次いで農民、職人、そして商人を最下位に置いた。階級間の婚姻や職業の変更、階級間の移動、あるいは転居に至るまで、あらゆる種類の社会的活動が禁止されたり、厳しく制限されたりした。これが実現したのは、詳細な戸籍制度のためであるが、取り締まっていたのは奉行である。将軍はまた、連帯責任のルールを強化した。つまり、罪を犯した場合、犯人だけではなくその家族や、時には隣人までもが訴追されたのである。

19. 鎖国

　徳川将軍の戦略は、その後の日本史に多大な影響を与えた。儒教は大和時代後期より日本に伝わっていたが、徳川幕府の支配者たちは新儒学を採用し、封建的社会制度の強化に利用した。新儒学は侍社会に急速に浸透し、基本的な道徳を定めるとともに行動規範を提供した。事実、新儒学

once by fires, including the firebombing during World War II. The site of the original Edo Castle is the location of the current Imperial Palace.

The shogun also established a representative office in Kyoto to keep an eye on the activities of the imperial court, even though, in theory, the emperor was regarded as a divinity. As part of its authoritarian strategy, the Tokugawa shogunate owned approximately 25% of available land in Japan, dispersing the rest of it among the lords. These feudal domains were called *han*.

To create social stability, Ieyasu also tightened class structure along Confucianist lines. He divided the nation into four classes, with samurai being the highest, then farmers, craftsmen, and merchants as the lowest. All manner of social activities, such as intermarriage between classes, the changing of jobs, movement from one class to another, or even relocating were either prohibited or strictly controlled. This was accomplished by means of a detailed registration system and enforced by the police. The shogun also strengthened the rule of group accountability—in other words, if a crime was committed, not only the perpetrator but also his or her family and sometimes even neighbors were prosecuted.

19. Closing the Nation

Overall, Tokugawa strategy had a huge impact on subsequent Japanese history. While Confucianism was known in Japan from the late Yamato Period, the Tokugawa rulers adopted its Neo-Confucian form to bolster the feudal social system. It was accepted rapidly by samurai society to undergird basic morality and provide models of behavior. In fact,

第4章 将軍と鎖国

は社会的安定の創設と維持に欠かせない道具となったのである。

特に、階級やヒエラルキーの感覚、中央集権政府や官僚制への信頼、あるいは集団主義的行動は、より個人主義的な欧米と比べて、現在でも日本の階級的、社会的価値観における重要な要素となっている。現在でも、公私を問わず目下の者が大失敗や罪を犯すと、目上の者も責任を問われるのが、その格好の例である。

現代の日本人の精神に最も深い影響を与えたのは、鎖国の時代である。徳川幕府は1639年、オランダ、中国、朝鮮の使節を除き、外国への門戸を閉ざした。交流を許された三か国ですら、長崎の出島と呼ばれる小さな人工島に押し込められていた。この政策は、欧米諸国の領土的野心に対し将軍が懸念を抱いたことによるものである。加えて、キリスト教が急速に広がりを見せていたことにより、将軍は、キリスト教が欧米による日本の植民地化の先兵になるのではとおそれたのだった。

17世紀初めには、オランダとイギリスは貿易活動をアジアに広げていた。スペインとポルトガルは、アジア諸国との貿易や宗教的関係を促進するべく、それぞれマニラとマカオに拠点を定めていた。両国はいずれも、日本国内で大きな存在感を示していた。しかし、オランダ人やイギリス人は、カトリックのスペイン人やポルトガル人とは違うアプローチをした。貿易にのみ関心を示し、宣教は行わなかったのである。オランダ人やイギリス人たちは、カトリック教徒たち

出島でオランダ船の入港を見守る
オランダ人商人
Dutch trader watching an incoming Dutch ship at Dejima

Neo-Confucianism became an essential tool in establishing and maintaining social stability.

In particular, the sense of class, of hierarchy, of centralized government and bureaucracy, and of group-oriented behavior still remain as important structural and social values in Japan, distinguishing it from the more individualistic West. As a case in point, even now, whether in public affairs or private business, if a subordinate makes a serious mistake or commits a crime, his or her boss is considered to be responsible, too.

遊女を連れたオランダ人
Dutchmen with Courtesans

The most profound influence on modern Japanese mentality stems from the period of Japan's isolation from the rest of the world. The Tokugawa shogunate closed Japan's door to foreign countries in 1639, except for Dutch, Chinese, and Korean envoys. Even they were restricted to the small artificial island called Dejima in Nagasaki. This policy was inspired by the shogunate's concern over the territorial ambitions of Western nations. In addition, with Christianity's rapid growth, the shogunate feared that Christianity was the advance guard of a Western plot to colonize Japan.

By the beginning of the seventeenth century, the Dutch and British had begun to expand their trading activities in Asia. The Spanish and Portuguese had opened headquarters in Manila and Macao, respectively, to promote trade and religious relationships with Asians. Both countries had a big presence in Japan. The Dutch and British, however, took a different approach from their Catholic rivals, because they were interested solely in trade, not in missionary work. They persuaded the

を国外追放するよう徳川政府に働きかけた。しかし、イギリスは日本は利益にならないと考えて、西九州の平戸にあった貿易拠点を1623年に閉鎖した。

徳川将軍は、キリスト教を断固として禁止した。キリスト教に改宗した無数の日本人が、信仰を捨てるまで迫害された。こうしたキリスト教徒の迫害は、1637年に劇的なクライマックスを迎えることとなる。キリスト教信者や重税に苦しむ農民たちが、長崎近くの島原で反乱を起こしたのである。この反乱は6か月ほど続き、将軍は鎮圧のために10万余の軍勢を派遣した。

反乱の後、将軍は弾圧を強化して、交易していたカトリック諸国に対する態度を硬化した。ポルトガル人は1639年に追放され、海外在住の日本人は帰国を禁じられた。17世紀初めの20年間には、多くの日本人が東南アジアへと出航し、日本人集落を築いて現地やヨーロッパ人の商人と交易をしていた。仙台の伊達氏をはじめ、欧州に使節を派遣した大名もいた。こうした活動は、1639年に鎖国政策が発布されると厳しく禁じられた。1854年に幕府がアメリカのマシュー・ペリー司令官率いる黒船の圧力に負けて門戸を開くまで、この鎖国政策は続くことになる。

この鎖国政策がもたらした最も明白な利点は、徳川家による政治社会制度が200年強にわたり安定して続いたことであった。しかし、その不利益も広範囲に及んだ。日本は西洋諸国に比べて工業の面で大いに劣ることとなり、追いつくことがほぼ不可能になったのである。日本はこの代償を、19世紀後半から20世紀にかけて支払うこととなる。さらに深いレベルでは、日本人は長い鎖国を経て、自らが独自の存在であるという複雑な観念を抱くようになった。自分たちは島国の同質的な人種であり、他の全ての人種と異なる

Tokugawa government to evict their Catholic rivals from the country. In the end, however, the British found Japan unprofitable and closed their trading post, located in Hirado in western Kyushu, in 1623.

The shogunate was unrelenting in its prohibition of Christianity. Countless Japanese converts faced martyrdom unless they recanted. The persecutions of Christians came to a dramatic climax in 1637, when Christian followers and farmers, suffering under a heavy tax burden, rebelled in Shimabara, near Nagasaki. This rebellion lasted about six months, and the shogunate dispatched over a hundred thousand soldiers to quell it.

After the rebellion, the shogunate intensified persecution and took a stronger stand against its Catholic trading partners. The Portuguese were ejected in 1639, and all Japanese living abroad were prohibited from returning home. During the first two decades of the seventeenth century, many Japanese sailed to Southeast Asia to create Japanese settlements and conduct trade with local and European merchants. Some lords, like Date of Sendai, sent envoys to the West. All such activities were strictly prohibited when the seclusion policy was promulgated in 1639. This policy continued until 1854, when the shogunate opened Japan's door under the pressure of American Commodore Matthew Perry and his black-hulled ships.

The most obvious benefit of the seclusion policy was the stability of the Tokugawa political and social institutions for more than two hundred years. Its drawback, however, was also far-reaching: industrially, Japan fell so far behind Western countries that it was almost impossible to catch up. Japan paid the price for this in the latter half of the nineteenth and in the twentieth century. Even more profound, this long seclusion gave the Japanese a complex sense of their own uniqueness—that they were a homogeneous island race different from all other peoples. This

存在であるという考え方である。この信念は今日なお日本に見られ、日本人がグローバルなコミュニケーションをとれない理由として言及されることも多い。

20. 歌舞伎と浮世絵の時代

　鎖国政策と徳川幕府の安定政権の下で、日本の国内は発展した。都市は栄え、商人階級により貨幣経済が発展した。18世紀初めの江戸は、100万人を超える人々が住む、世界で最も人口の多い都市であった。

　裕福な商人や活発な経済に支えられて、芸術はこれまでにない高みに到達した。17世紀末頃には歌舞伎（大規模で様式化された、俳優中心の演劇）が出現し、洗練された演劇となった。歌舞伎俳優や都市の生活、あるいは自然美を称揚するべく、木版画が広く流通し、浮世絵という名の芸術として認められるようになった。19世紀末、これらの版画はフランスの印象派画家に深く影響を与えた。

　鈴木春信が1765年に木版多色摺りを発明すると、商業芸術としての浮世絵はさらに進展した。18世紀から19世紀初頭にかけて特に人気のあった浮世絵師には、喜多川歌麿や葛飾北斎、東洲斎写楽らがいる。書籍の出版も活発に行われた。侍が主人公の恋愛小説や悲劇が広く流布し、歌舞伎や人形浄瑠璃である文楽のために翻案された。

　江戸時代における文化的活動の最盛期は二回あった。一回目は17世紀末、第五代徳川将軍綱吉の治世に始まるもので、元禄時代と呼ばれている。元禄時代は比較的豊かな時

Chapter 4: Shogun and Seclusion

conviction persists in Japan today and is often cited as a reason for the Japanese inability to communicate globally.

20. The Period of Kabuki and Ukiyo-e

Under the seclusion policy and stable Tokugawa rule, Japan enjoyed domestic prosperity. Cities prospered and the merchant class developed a money-based economy. Around the beginning of the eighteenth century, more than one million people lived in Edo, making it the world's most populous city.

Supported by wealthy merchants and a vigorous economy, the arts reached unprecedented heights. Kabuki (grand, stylized, actor-centered drama) emerged to become a sophisticated performing art around the end of the seventeenth century. To celebrate Kabuki actors, city life, and the beauties of nature, woodblock brochures were widely circulated and became recognized as an art form called *ukiyo-e*. In the late nineteenth century, these prints had a profound impact on French impressionists.

With the invention of color woodblock printing in 1765 by Suzuki Harunobu, *ukiyo-e* made further advances as a commercial art. Kitagawa Utamaro, Katsushika Hokusai, and Toshusai Sharaku were among the most popular artists in the eighteenth and early nineteenth centuries. Book publishing was also quite active. Love stories and tragic tales with samurai heroes were widely circulated and adapted for Kabuki and the Bunraku puppet theater.

Edo period cultural activity had two peaks. The first began toward

第4章 将軍と鎖国

松尾芭蕉
Matsuo Basho

代であった。平和な時代が続き、侍の武芸は次第に求められなくなっていった。侍の多くは役人の職を得て、伝統的な武士と比べて奢侈な生活を好むようになった。この傾向は、江戸の新興中流階級にも等しく見られた。元禄時代は、十七音の俳句が始まった時代でもある。松尾芭蕉は、俳句の達人としてよく知られている。

江戸時代の二回目の文化的最盛期は18世紀末の文化・文政期である。この時期には、江戸に加えて関西（大阪と京都を含む地域）においても文化活動が栄えた。たとえば、脚本家の近松門左衛門は関西を拠点にして、よく知られた多くの物語を文楽や歌舞伎に翻案した。またこの時期、西洋の船が日本列島の沿岸に出没して扉をたたき始めた。これにより一部の学者は長崎に出向き、オランダ人を介して西洋文化を学んだ。

喜多川歌麿「汗を拭く女」
"Woman wiping Perspiration,"
by Kitagawa Utamaro

菱川師宣「見返り美人」
"Beauty looking back," by
Hishikawa Moronobu

the end of the seventeenth century during the years of the fifth Tokugawa shogun, Tsunayoshi, and was called the Genroku era. It was a time of relative prosperity. Thanks to the Pax Tokugawa, the martial skills of the samurai became less and less in demand. Many samurai took jobs as civil servants and came to prefer a relatively more extravagant lifestyle compared to the traditional warrior. This trend coincided with the burgeoning middle-class life of Edo. The Genroku era also saw the emergence of *haiku*, the seventeen-syllable poem. Matsuo Basho is well-known as the master of this poetic form.

The second cultural peak in the Edo Period occurred in the late eighteenth century, the Bunka-Bunsei era. Cultural activity thrived not only in Edo but also in Kansai (the area including Osaka and Kyoto.) For example, the playwright Chikamatsu Monzaemon adapted many famous stories for Bunraku and Kabuki in the Kansai area. It was also around this time that Western ships began to appear along the coasts to knock on the door of insular Japan. This eventually stimulated some scholars to travel to Nagasaki, where they could study Western culture through the medium of Dutch.

歌川国貞の浮世絵に描かれた歌舞伎俳優
Kabuki actors depicted in an ukiyo-e by Utagawa Kunisada

21. 封建制度の衰退

　18世紀後半には、徳川政府が生み出した社会制度は、特に経済の面で崩壊の兆候を示し始めた。大都市はすでに貨幣制度に基づいて動いていたが、大名たちは領民が栽培した米により徴税し、侍の給料も米で支払われた。その結果、侍は生きるために米を貨幣と交換する必要があった。事実、都市の商人たちが大名や侍に融資するのが慣例となりつつあり、武士たちは皮肉にも、徳川幕府の封建制度では最下位であると考えられていた商人階級から金を借りることとなった。

　徳川幕府は、大名にさらなる重圧を課していた。その一つに参勤交代がある。表向きは警護上の理由で、全ての大名は一年ごとに江戸に住まわなければならなかったのである。毎年江戸と領地を往復するだけでも多額の負担を要したが、これに加えて、大名たちは江戸と藩の両方に住居を構えなければならなかった。

徳川吉宗（1684–1751）。徳川幕府第八代将軍。享保の改革と呼ばれる大きな改革に着手し、江戸後期の財政危機からの立て直しを図った

Tokugawa Yoshimune (1684–1751), the eighth shogun of the Tokugawa shogunate, undertook the big reform, Kyoho no Kaikaku, to save the financial crisis in late Edo

　多くの大名は、さまざまな手段を講じて財政状況を改善しようとした。たとえば薩摩藩（現鹿児島県）は、沖縄を介して密かに外国貿易を行っていた。他方、重税に抗議する百姓一揆にあって失脚する大名も多かった。徳川幕府の政策により、職や住処すら失った侍も多かったのである。

　江戸時代を通じて、農民階級は酷使され、軽視された。農民たちは翌年まで生き延びるだけの作物しか手元に置くことを許されず、残りは年貢として

21. Decline of the Feudal System

Around the latter part of the eighteenth century, the social system created by the Tokugawa started to show signs of decay, particularly in the economy. Big cities were already operating on a currency-based system, while domain lords were receiving taxes in the form of rice grown by their vassals. Samurai salaries were also paid in rice. As a result, the samurai needed to exchange rice for money in order to survive. In fact, it was becoming quite common for city merchants to finance both lords and their samurai, who eventually became indebted to the merchants, who were ironically considered the lowest social class in the Tokugawa feudal system.

Rural lords shouldered additional burdens imposed by the shogunate. One of these was the *sankin kotai*, which required all lords, ostensibly for security reasons, to reside in Edo every other year. Traveling to Edo and back to their home province each year was exorbitantly expensive. Adding to this expense was the cost of maintaining two residences, one in Edo and the other in their home province or *han*.

Many lords tried to improve their financial situation through various means. For example, the Satsuma *han*, now Kagoshima prefecture, secretly conducted foreign trade through Okinawa. On the other hand, many lords simply failed, faced with rebellious farmers who protested against heavy taxes. In fact, many samurai became jobless or even homeless as a result of Tokugawa policy.

松平定信（1759–1829）。徳川幕府における財政改革（寛政の改革）で知られている

Matsudaira Sadanobu (1759–1829), famous for his financial, Kansei no Kaikaku, for Tokugawa Shogunate

The peasant farmers were abused and neglected as a class throughout the

第4章 将軍と鎖国

　納めなければならなかった。そればかりか、農民は江戸時代全体にわたり、飢饉に苦しめられていた。特に、1732年、1783年、1833年の三回の飢饉は、ひどい苦しみをもたらした。その結果、農民の反乱や一揆が珍しくなかったのもうなずける。

　徳川将軍は江戸時代の最初期より、関ヶ原の戦い以後に徳川家に忠誠を誓った大名たちが問題を起こす可能性があることをおそれ、こうした外様大名の生活をとりわけ困窮させた。最終的には、外様大名たちの多くは領地を奪われ、仕えていた多くの侍は収入の道を断たれた。職を失った侍は浪人と呼ばれたが、浪人たちが巷にあふれるようになった。一番上の階級であるはずの侍が厳しい財政難に陥ったのは、徳川時代における根本的な社会的矛盾であった。強力な商人階級の台頭、多数の浪人、絶え間ない百姓一揆により、徳川政権は内から大きく蝕まれていった。この矛盾は、外国軍艦の出現というもう一つの難問によりさらに複雑になった。

浮世絵「東海道五十三次」より「日本橋」。封建制度の崩壊に伴い、商人の町が栄えた

Ukiyo-e of Nihonbashi from The Fifty-three Stations of the Tokaido. While declining the feudal system, the merchant town were prospered

Tokugawa Period. They were allowed to keep just enough of their harvests to stay alive until the next year—the rest of the produce was taken as tax. If this were not enough, peasants were plagued by famine throughout this era. The three famines of 1732, 1783, and 1833 in particular caused intense suffering. As a result, it is no wonder that peasant uprisings and rebellions were not uncommon.

From the very beginning of the Tokugawa era, the shogunate sensed potential problems with those lords who swore allegiance to the Tokugawa only after the Battle of Sekigahara, and made their lives particularly difficult. In the end, many of these lords were stripped of their territory, leaving the thousands of samurai who served them without a livelihood. Such jobless samurai were called *ronin*, and they were ubiquitous. For the samurai, who occupied the highest social rank, to be in dire financial straits created a basic contradiction in Tokugawa society. The growing, powerful merchant class, large numbers of unemployed samurai, and continuous peasant rebellions created major internal anomalies for the Tokugawa rulers. This contradiction was compounded by another challenge: the appearance of foreign warships.

22. 開国と倒幕

　18世紀になると、日本の水域に多くの外国船が出現し、貿易の推進を試みた。徳川幕府は頑として鎖国を堅持した。しかし、マシュー・ペリー提督率いるアメリカのフリゲート艦4隻が1853年に江戸近くの浦賀湾に出現すると、徳川幕府は突如として、世界が日本を放置していた間、自分たちが泰平の眠りに就いていたことに気づいたのである。

　先進的な武器を備えた4隻の巨大戦艦が出現したことにより、幕府は政策の変更を余儀なくされた。長い交渉を経て、徳川幕府は1854年、ついに開国を決意した。少数の港への寄港を外国人に許可し、初めはアメリカ合衆国、次いでロシア、フランス、イギリス、オランダとの通商関係を樹立したのである。

ペリーの「黒船」
Perry's "Black Ships"

　国粋主義者の多くは、この方針転換を非難した。これほど大きな決断は朝廷に諮ることなしに実施するべきではなく、実際の政治権力はまだ幕府の手中にあるとしても、天皇を日本の最高統治者として尊重するべきであると考えたからである。多くの侍や、一部の大名すらも国粋主義的思想を持ち、「夷狄の圧力」に抵抗するよう幕府に働きかけた。

マシュー・ペリー総督
Commodore Matthew Perry

　幕府は、欧米諸国が優れた軍事力と科学技術を用いてアジア諸国を植民地化していることを十分に認識しており、そのため政策転換に反対する者を抑圧しようとした。これにより、幕府の新しい外交政策に反対する攘夷派と、佐幕派の二つの勢力に国内が二分した。朝廷のある京都は、権力闘争の中核となった。

22. Opening of the Nation and the Fall of the Tokugawa

In the eighteenth century, a number of foreign ships appeared in Japanese waters and attempted to instigate trade relations. But the shogunate stubbornly adhered to seclusion. However, when four U.S. frigates commanded by Commodore Matthew Perry arrived in Uraga Bay near Edo in 1853, the shogunate suddenly realized that it had been sleeping while the world passed them by.

Four huge warships with advanced weaponry were quite enough to convince the shogunate to modify its policies. After lengthy negotiations, the Tokugawa leaders finally decided to open the country's doors in 1854. They allowed foreign access to several ports and started trade relationships, first with the United States and then with Russia, France, England, and the Netherlands.

This policy reversal was condemned by many Japanese nationalists, who believed that a decision of this magnitude should not be made without consulting the imperial court. They thought the emperor should be respected as Japan's supreme ruler, even though actual administrative power was still in the hands of the shogunate. Many samurai and even some lords held nationalist views and strongly urged the shogunate to resist "barbarian pressure."

The shogunate was fully aware that Western countries were colonizing Asian lands by means of their advanced military power and technology, and consequently it strove to suppress those opposed to its shift in policy. Thus, the nation was divided into two camps: those who opposed the shogunate's new foreign policy and those who supported it. Kyoto, where the imperial court was located, became the center of this struggle for power.

第4章　将軍と鎖国

　政治的影響力の点では、薩摩藩（九州南部、現鹿児島県）と長州藩（本州西部、現山口県）が最有力の藩となった。遠くない将来に、薩摩藩と長州藩は有能な若い侍たちを明治政府の要職に送り込むことに成功する。彼らは、日本の近代化を推進する新しい指導者であった。しかし、両藩ははじめ外国の影響を日本から追いやろうと試み、欧米列強と戦った。しかし欧米の海軍が反撃に成功すると、薩摩と長州は、先進的な軍事力や科学技術を取り入れて発展させる必要があることを学んだのである。

　その後、薩摩藩と長州藩は旧体制を覆す企てに加わった。一連の戦いや暗殺などの波瀾を経て、1866年に両藩は手を結び、薩長同盟を結成して徳川政権に対抗した。朝廷は密かにこの同盟を支援していた。この同盟の仲立ちとなったのは、土佐（南四国、現高知県）の坂本龍馬である。もっとも坂本龍馬は、この密約が成った後に残念ながら暗殺された。一方の幕府は、こうした新しい動きに対抗するだけの経済力や軍事力を有していなかった。

最後の徳川将軍、徳川慶喜
The last Tokugawa shogun, Tokugawa Yoshinobu

　大きな圧力の下で、最後の将軍徳川慶喜は1867年に将軍職を辞した。この時、反徳川勢力は朝廷の下で新政府を樹立しようと試みていた。しかし慶喜は、戦わずして退こうとはしなかった。大政奉還後、慶喜は軍勢を大坂城に集結して、薩摩藩の有力な新指導者の一人であった西郷隆盛率いる反徳川同盟に対抗しようとした。しかし1868年、西郷は京都近郊の鳥羽伏見の戦いで徳川軍を破った。江戸に逃亡した慶喜は降伏し、こうして封建時代は終わりを告げた。

94

In terms of political influence, Satsuma (now Kagoshima prefecture, located in southern Kyushu) and Choshu (now Yamaguchi prefecture, located in western Honshu) had become the most influential domains. In the not-too-distant future Satsuma and Choshu would successfully promote talented young samurai into influential positions in the new Meiji government. These were the new leaders who would launch Japan on its modern trajectory. Initially, however, the two domains tried to remove foreign influence from Japan and even engaged the Western powers in battle. When the Western navies successfully counterattacked, they learned the necessity of developing advanced military power and technology.

Subsequently, Satsuma and Choshu led the effort to overthrow the old regime. After a series of battles, assassinations, and other tumultuous events, these two domains joined hands in 1866 to create an allied front against the Tokugawa, secretly supported by the imperial court. The coordinator of this alliance was Sakamoto Ryoma of Tosa (now Kochi prefecture in southern Shikoku), who was unfortunately assassinated after this secret agreement was made. The shogun was too weak economically and militarily to withstand the new movement.

Under immense pressure, Tokugawa Yoshinobu, the last shogun, resigned in 1867. At that point, the anti-Tokugawa forces attempted to establish a new government under the aegis of the imperial court. But Yoshinobu did not give up without a fight. After resigning, he concentrated his forces at Osaka Castle to oppose the anti-Tokugawa alliance led by Saigo Takamori, one of the distinguished new leaders from Satsuma. By 1868, Saigo had defeated the Tokugawa forces in the Kyoto suburbs of Toba and Fushimi. After escaping to Edo, Yoshinobu surrendered, bringing the feudal era to an end.

第5章 明治時代

23. 明治維新

　1868年は、日本近代史における最も重要な年の一つである。この年、日本は公式に近代国家として出発した。新しい天皇親政体制は、依然として徳川家に忠誠を誓っていたほぼ全ての対抗勢力を一掃した。しかし、徳川慶喜の降伏後に執拗な抵抗を試みた大名もいた。新政府と徳川政権の支持勢力との一連の戦いは、一括りに戊辰戦争と呼ばれている。最もよく知られた戦いは東北の会津若松で行われ、多数の侍が死傷した。1869年4月、最後の親徳川派が北海道・箱館の戦いで敗れた。

明治天皇
Emperor Meiji

　新政府は、朝廷を京都から江戸に遷し、江戸を東京（東の都）と改称することとした。新政府の果たすべき役割は明らかだった。日本を強力な軍事力と強固な産業基盤を備えた先進国へと変えていくことである。孝明天皇が1866年に崩御し、明治天皇が1867年9月に正式に即位した。これを明治維新という。

　内政的にも国際的にも、安定した政権が必要とされていた。他の多くのアジア諸国がたどった、欧米列強による植民地化の運命を避けるため、日本の新指導者たちは近代的な技術、軍事力、さらには行政組織を作り出す必要があった。国内

大久保利通
Toshimichi Okubo

西郷隆盛
Takamori Saigo

Chapter 5:
The Meiji Period

23. Meiji Restoration

The year 1868 is one of the most important in modern Japanese history. It was the year Japan officially set out to become a modern state. The new imperial government had swept away nearly all opposition forces still loyal to the Tokugawa shogunate. But as Tokugawa

戊辰戦争では、長州藩の侍が
会津侍と戦った
During the Bosin War, samurai of the Choshu clan fought against Aizu Samurai

Yoshinobu surrendered, some lords persistently tried to fight back. A series of battles between the new government and the Tokugawa supporters ensued, which is collectively referred to as the Boshin War. The most famous battle took place in Aizu-Wakamatsu in Tohoku, where many samurai were killed and wounded. By April 1869, the last of the Tokugawa supporters was defeated in Hakodate, Hokkaido.

The new government decided to move the imperial court from Kyoto to Edo, which was renamed Tokyo (Eastern Capital). The task of the new government was obvious: to transform Japan into an advanced nation with a strong military and a robust industrial base. When the Emperor Komei died in 1866, the Emperor Meiji officially succeeded to the throne in September 1867. This is known as the Meiji Restoration.

A stable government was needed for both domestic and international reasons. To avoid the fate of many other Asian nations, which had been colonized by Western powers, Japan's new leaders needed to

第5章 明治時代

では、木戸孝允、大久保利通、岩倉具視、先に述べた西郷隆盛らの先導の下で、社会階級制度や侍の特権が廃止された。

政府は一般市民の徴兵を開始した。中央集権化を図るため、古い封建的な藩は廃止され、県の制度が導入されて東京から知事が任命されることとなった。古い金融制度も近代的な銀行制度や貨幣制度に変更された。新しい税制や法制度も中央政府の下で統合され、鉄道、遠距離通信、郵便制度も確立した。1872年、初の鉄道が東京〜横浜間で開通した。これらはみな、欧米に追いつき、自国とその権益を守るという政府の使命を実現するための重要な施策であった。

結局、日本は欧米との遭遇により、自らのアイデンティティをさらに自覚するようになった。明治維新の前、日本は230年以上にわたり鎖国政策を取っていたが、その間に独特の価値観や道徳を発展させてきた。しかし今や、世界に門戸を開き、順応していかなければならなくなったのである。そこで新指導者たちは、外国の科学技術をそれに付随する価値観や世界観とともに輸入し、改革を開始した。新しい要素と伝統との混合により、日本は前進する機会を手にすることとなった。振り返ってみると、明治時代は、国粋主義を生み出した運命と機会のるつぼがもたらしたものであり、第二次世界大戦へと続く道の出発点でもあった。

create modern technology, military power, and administrative systems. Domestically, social class distinctions and samurai privileges were abolished under the leadership of Takayoshi Kido, Toshimichi Okubo, Tomomi Iwakura, the previously mention Takamori Saigo, and others.

The government began to conscript soldiers from among ordinary citizens. To create centralized authority, it abolished the old feudal domains and introduced a system of prefectures with governors appointed by Tokyo. The old financial system was converted to a modern banking and monetary system. New tax and legal policies were integrated under the central government. Railroads, telecommunications, and postal systems were established. The first rail service opened in 1872 between Tokyo and Yokohama. All these were important steps toward realizing the government's mission to overtake the West and protect the nation and its interests.

In end result, the encounter with the West caused Japan to gain a better sense of its own identity. Before the Meiji Restoration, Japan had been isolated for more than 230 years—a period during which it had developed a distinctive set of values and ethics. Now Japan was open to the world and had to adapt. The new leadership began its reforms by importing foreign technology with its attendant values and worldview. The mixture of the new with the traditional provided Japan with an opportunity to move forward. In retrospect, the Meiji Period also marked the starting point down the road to World War II, the result of a crucible of fate and opportunity that produced nationalism.

1872年、新橋と横浜とを結ぶ初の蒸気機関車が開通した
In 1872, the first steam train between Shinbashi and Yokohama was opened

24. 西南戦争から明治憲法の発布まで

　近代国家を築きあげる上で、明治政府には克服すべき課題があった。最重要課題は、特権を失った元武士たちの不満を和らげることであった。政府への反乱を企てる武士も多かった。1877年の西南戦争は、きわめて深刻な内戦であった。これは明治維新の立役者の一人であった西郷隆盛が政治的見解の違いから政府を去ったことが契機となり、西郷の信奉者や元武士の不満分子らが西郷を焚きつけて蜂起させたものである。西郷の私兵は最終的には三万人を超えていた。反乱ははじめ鹿児島（旧薩摩藩、西郷の故郷）で始まり、九州南部に広がった。しかし数か月後、東京より派遣された強力な近代軍の前に西郷は圧倒され、最後は鹿児島で自刃する。

　西南戦争の後、侍の不満分子は武器を取る代わりに声を上げて抗議を続けた。彼らは政府に要求を聞くよう求め、欧米諸国に見られる代表民主制を導入しないことを批判した。

西南戦争、田原坂の戦い
Battle of Tabaruzaka in the Seinan War

24. From the Seinan War to the Promulgation of the Meiji Constitution

To forge a modern nation, the Meiji government needed to overcome several challenges. The most important was to assuage the frustration of former samurai who had lost their privileges. Many of them tried to foment rebellion against the government. The Seinan War in 1877 was their most serious effort. It was sparked when Takamori Saigo, one of the heroes of the Meiji Restoration, left the government over stark political differences. His followers and many frustrated samurai pressed Saigo to rebel. His private army eventually numbered more than thirty thousand. Their rebellion started in Kagoshima (formerly Satsuma, Saigo's homeland) and spread throughout the southern part of Kyushu. However, within several months Saigo was overwhelmed by the powerful modern army dispatched from Tokyo, and he committed suicide in Kagoshima.

After the Seinan War, discontented samurai continued their protests with their voices instead of weapons. They asked the government to listen to their demands. They criticized it for not introducing representative democracy such as found in Western nations.

明治憲法の発布
Meiji Constitution promulgation

しかし明治政府は、この種の抗議をさらなる不満の種を宿すものとして危険視した。政府の目的は、天皇の権威の下に近代的な行政、司法、立法府を創設することであった。内部の混乱や議論が広く見られたものの、政府は1889年、ついに議会制度を導入し、ドイツ憲法を手本とした憲法を制定した。翌年、最初の帝国議会が開会した。すでに1885年に内閣が創設され、伊藤博文が最初の総理大臣に任命されていた。

この議会制度は、いくつかの点で民主主義とは言い切れなかった。参政権は税を支払っている男性にのみ与えられ、さらに上院は、華族や皇族、および天皇が任命した者のみで構成されていた。明治憲法の下では帝国議会は天皇にのみ責任を負い、天皇が最高権力者であった。憲法が制定されると、政府はヨーロッパ（今回はフランス）を手本に刑法と民法を制定した。

この頃には経済が上向きになり始め、製造業もかつてないほどに成長した。特に繊維と造船が活況を呈していたが、こうした成功は基本的に、豊かな特権階級を政府が強力に後押ししたためであり、大部分の平民や農民は相変わらず貧しかった。そのため、国会制度を制定する紆余曲折の段階で社会主義運動が勢いを増した。政府は、こうした反逆分子を最初は弾圧したが、のちに外国との戦争や侵略により目先をそらそうとした。

The Meiji government, however, considered such protests dangerous, embodying the seeds of further discontent. The government's aim was to create modern administrative, judicial and legislative powers under the authority of the emperor. After extensive internal confusion and argument, they finally installed a parliamentary system in 1889 with a constitution modeled after Germany's. The first imperial parliament, called the Diet, was opened the next year. The cabinet had already been created in 1885, with Hirobumi Ito appointed as the first prime minister.

In several respects, this parliamentary system was not completely democratic. Suffrage was granted only to tax-paying males. The upper house of the Diet was made up exclusively of aristocrats, the emperor's relatives, and individuals appointed by the emperor. The constitution made the Diet responsible solely to the emperor, who was considered the supreme authority. As it had done with the constitution, the government followed a European model—France—for its criminal and civil law.

Around the same time, the economy began to heat up, and manufacturing hit new heights. Particularly vigorous were the textile and shipping industries. However, these successes were largely due to strong governmental support of the wealthy privileged classes. Almost all ordinary citizens and farmers remained poor. As a result, during the tortuous attempts to create a parliamentary system, socialist movements gained momentum. The government first tried to deal with such recalcitrant elements by oppression and later by shifting attention to foreign wars and invasion.

25. 日露戦争への道

　19世紀は帝国主義の時代だった。イギリス、フランス、ドイツ、ロシア、オランダ、のちにアメリカが主要プレーヤーとなって外国の領域を占領し、アジア・アフリカ諸国に影響圏を築きあげた。これら欧米諸国は日本と不平等条約を結び、日本の主権を制限した。明治時代の最初期より、日本政府の主な仕事はこうした不平等な状態を解消することであったが、完全な平等が回復したのは、日本が世界の軍事大国であると認められてからである。

　日本は、地理的に近接しているロシアを最大の脅威と見ていた。したがって日本は、まず朝鮮半島に目を向けた。朝鮮は清王朝の属国とみなされていたが、朝鮮に強力な影響力を及ぼすことがロシアから自国の権益を守る最上の方法であると考えたのである。そこで、日本は朝鮮に対し、通商を求めて開港を要求したあと不平等条約を押しつけ、最終的には朝鮮の内政を操って、日本軍の駐留を認めさせた。こうした動きにより、清との8か月に及ぶ戦争（日清戦争）が勃発したが、欧米式を採用した日本軍がたやすく勝利を収めた。

　1895年の下関条約において、清は台湾をはじめとするさまざまな島や遼東半島を日本に割譲し、日本に戦時補償金を支払った。しかし、清国内にそれぞれ勢力範囲や資産を有していた欧米諸国は、日本の勝利を脅威とみなし、ロシア、ドイツ、フランスは遼東半島を清に返還するよう要求した。こうした西洋列強と敵対するのは危険過ぎると考えた日本は、嫌々ながらこの要求を呑んだ。

　しかし、日本政府はこうした不当な国際的圧力を利用して、国内の世論をナショナリズムへと導いた。軍事投資を

25. Way to the Russo-Japanese War

The nineteenth century was the era of imperialism. England, France, Germany, Russia, the Netherlands, and later the United States were the major players in occupying foreign territory and creating spheres of influence in Asian and African nations. These Western nations concluded unequal treaties with Japan, curtailing its sovereignty. From the very beginning of the Meiji Period, the government's main task was to rectify these unfair conditions. Balance was not completely restored until Japan was recognized as a global military power.

Japan viewed Russia as its most serious threat because of its geographical proximity. Accordingly, it turned its attention first to the Korean Peninsula, for even though Korea was considered a tributary of the Qing Dynasty, the Japanese believed that strong influence in Korea would be the best way to protect Japanese interests from Russia. Thus, Japan demanded that Korea open its ports to trade, and then imposed its own unequal treaty. Finally, after manipulating Korea's internal politics, Japan forced it to accept a Japanese military presence. These activities provoked an eight-month war with China, which the Westernized Japanese military easily won.

In the Treaty of Shimonoseki of 1895 China ceded Taiwan, various other islands, and the Liao-dong Peninsula to Japan, and agreed to pay a war indemnity. However, Western nations, with their respective spheres of influence and assets in China, saw the Japanese victory as a threat. Eventually, Russia, Germany, and France demanded the restoration of the Liao-dong Peninsula to the Qing Dynasty. Japan reluctantly conceded to this demand, feeling it was too dangerous to have hostile relations with these three Western powers.

Still, the Japanese government used this unjustified international

第5章　明治時代

行い、工業化を推進するとともに、朝鮮への影響力を行使しようとし続けたのである。

19世紀末における東アジアの国際権力闘争には、清でさらなる経済的チャンスを求めていたほぼ全ての欧米列強が関わっていた。

イギリスは、日本がロシアの圧力を懸念していることを理解し、ロシアの領土的野心を排除するべく日本を支援することにした。日本とイギリスは1902年に同盟を結び、ロシアに対する共通の利害を公に表明した。アメリカもまた日本を支援した。1898年の米西戦争後にフィリピンを併合したアメリカは、今度は満州で経済的影響力を確立することを望んだためである。他方、イギリスのライバルであったフランスとドイツは、ロシアを支援した。

こうした複雑で込み入った関係を背景として、日本とロシアは、満州と朝鮮半島に権益を確立する上で重大な障害に直面した。ついに1904年2月、日本は10年間の準備の後、ロシアに宣戦布告した。ロシアは広大な領土、科学技術、強大な軍事力を備えた超大国の一つであり、明治政府は大きなリスクを負ってこの戦争に臨んだ。日本はロシアの陸海軍と多くの戦いで衝突し、その過程で経済資源が枯渇したが、英米は日本の戦いに多額の資金援助を行った。一方のロシア政府は、戦争を続けて軍事力や経済力が弱体化すると、ロシア国内で拡大しつつある革命分子の動きがさらに勢いづくのではないかとおそれた。

仁川湾のロシア戦艦ヴァリャーグ号（日露戦争時）
Russian Crusier Varyag in Chemulpo Bay during Russo-Japanese War

pressure to turn Japanese public opinion toward nationalism. They invested in the military and ramped up industrialization, and they continued their attempts to exercise influence in Korea.

The international power struggle in East Asia in the late nineteenth century involved nearly all the major Western countries seeking broader economic opportunities in China. When the British clearly grasped Japan's concern about Russia's pressure, they opted to support Japan in order to defuse Russian territorial ambitions. Japan and England became allied in 1902, making official their common interest against Russia. The United States also supported Japan, because, following their annexation of the Philippines after the Spanish-American War in 1898, they wanted to establish an economic presence in Manchuria. France and Germany, on the other hand, were British rivals and therefore supported Russia.

Given these difficult and complex relationships, Japan and Russia faced formidable obstacles in establishing their interests in Manchuria and the Korean Peninsula. Japan finally declared war on Russia in February 1904, after ten years of preparation. This war posed great risks for Meiji Japan, as Russia was one of the reigning superpowers with vast territories, technology, and military might. While Japan clashed with the Russian army and navy in a number of bloody battles and exhausted its economic resources in the process, its efforts were heavily financed by England and the United States. At the same time, the Russian government feared that if they continued the war and debilitated their military and economy, the growing revolutionary movement in Russia would gain further momentum.

そこでアメリカ大統領セオドア・ルーズベルトが講話条約を斡旋し、日本とロシアの使節団がアメリカのニューハンプシャー州ポーツマスに集結して交渉を行った。日本は南樺太と南満州鉄道の経営権を手にした。こうして、双方ともに多額の出費を要し、多数の死傷者を出した日露戦争は1905年に終結した。

26. 韓国併合

日露戦争の主戦場は中国であった。欧米列強と新たなプレーヤーである大日本帝国はアジアをチェス盤として用いたが、それもアジアの宿命であった。日本国内にもロシアにも、戦争に反対した者はいた。日本では、社会主義者やキリスト教活動家が重要な反戦運動を展開した。帝国主義に反対した著名な人物には、キリスト教思想家の内村鑑三と社会主義者の幸徳秋水らがいる。

しかし、大多数の日本人は日本の勝利に酔いしれたばかりでなく、思ったほどの戦果が得られなかったことに失望した。ロシアは日本が疲弊しており、戦争を続けるだけの財力がないことを見透かしていたため、日本側はポーツマスでの交渉で苦戦を強いられた。国民の失望を埋め合わせ、欧米列強による日本への尊敬を勝ち得るため、そして経済的安定と国の安全保障を取り戻すため、伊藤博文ら日本の指導者は、朝鮮の併合が不可欠であると考えた。

日露戦争が終わると、朝鮮は完全に日本の支配下に置かれた。朝鮮は国際社会に抗議したが、欧米列強は一切相手

American president Theodore Roosevelt offered to mediate a peace treaty. Delegations from Japan and Russia met in the United States at Portsmouth, New Hampshire, to negotiate. Japan was awarded southern Sakhalin and ownership of the South Manchuria Railway. Thus, the Russo-Japanese War came to an end in 1905, after costing huge sums of money and the loss of many lives on both sides.

26. Annexation of Korea

Japan and Russia fought their war mainly in China. It was the fate of Asia that Western powers and the new player, Imperial Japan, used Asia as their chessboard. There were people who opposed war in both Japan and Russia. In Japan, Socialists and Christian activists played an important antiwar role. The Christian philosopher Kanzo Uchimura and the Socialist activist Shusui Kotoku were the most well-known figures to speak out against imperialism.

However, the vast majority of Japanese were exhilarated over Japan's triumph but also disappointed that it did not gain as much from the war as expected. The negotiations in Portsmouth were challenging for the Japanese side, since the Russians knew Japan had exhausted its resources and couldn't afford to continue the war. To counter the Japanese disappointment, to elicit respect for Japan among the Western powers, and to recover economic stability and national security, Japanese leaders like Hirobumi Ito believed that the annexation of Korea was indispensable.

When the war against Russia ended, Korea was completely under Japanese control. Korea protested to the international community, but

にしなかった。そもそも欧米列強も、インドや中国、フィリピン、その他多くのアジア・アフリカ諸国で同様の帝国主義を展開していたのである。したがって、1910年に日本が朝鮮を併合したときも、欧米からの干渉や抗議はなかった。日本はアメリカによるフィリピン支配を承認していたため、アメリカは日本の行動を秘密裏に承認していた。伊藤博文が寺内正毅を初代朝鮮総督に任命し、朝鮮王朝は正式に滅亡した。

　日本による韓国併合は日本が第二次世界大戦に敗北するまで続いたが、深い爪痕を残した。日本の官憲は朝鮮の独立運動を厳しく弾圧し、拷問することもあった。1919年、最も有名な抗日運動である三・一運動が起こった。この運動は全国的に展開されて、二百万人を超える朝鮮人が参加した。日本国内でも、朝鮮人はしばしば差別の対象となった。第二次世界大戦時には、十万人を超える朝鮮人が強制労働のため日本に連れてこられた（海外で戦う兵士のための慰安婦もいた）。こうして日本に移ってきた朝鮮人移民は朝鮮の独立後も日本に住み続けており、今日に至るまで差別を受けている。

日本の歴史上初の総理大臣、
伊藤博文

Hirobumi Ito, a preeminent Japanese political leader and the first prime minister in Japanese history

Chapter 5: The Meiji Period

none of the Western powers responded. After all, they had undertaken similar imperialist activities in India, China, the Philippines, and many other Asian and African countries. Therefore, when the Japanese finally colonized Korea in 1910, there was no interference or protest from the West. The United States secretly approved of Japan's actions, because Japan had approved of the U.S. control of the Philippines. When Hirobumi Ito appointed Masatake Terauchi as the first governor of Korea, the Korean kingdom officially ceased to exist.

The Japanese annexation of Korea, which lasted until Japan's defeat in World War II, left deep scars. Japanese officials responded to Korean independence movements with harsh persecution, even torture. The most famous incident, the March First Movement, occurred in 1919. This was a massive, nationwide anti-Japanese demonstration in which over two million Koreans participated. In Japan, too, Koreans were often the target of discrimination. During World War II, over a hundred thousand Koreans were forced to relocate to Japan as laborers (and sometimes as prostitutes for the military fighting abroad). Many such Korean immigrants have continued living in Japan even after Korea's independence, and they continue to face discrimination to this day.

韓国、漢城(現ソウル)の韓国統監府
Japanese General Government Building at Waeseongdae, Korea

安重根。1909年10月に伊藤博文を暗殺した韓国の義士

An Jung-geun. The Korean patriot who assassinated Hirobumi Ito in October of 1909

III

27. 明治時代の文化的動向

明治時代は近代日本の幕開けを告げた。日本は、技術的にも社会的にも進歩した欧米諸国の水準に追いつこうと鋭意努力しており、新たな教育、軍事、政府、行政制度の発展に重点的に投資した。1912年に明治時代が終わりを告げる頃には、欧米の影響は日本のあらゆる場所で見られたが、特に大都市では、建築から日常生活まで全てが欧米風になっていった。同時に、新たな文化的動向も数多く生まれていた。

夏目漱石
Soseki Natsume

これは、文学や芸術において最も顕著であった。たとえば、ロンドンに留学した夏目漱石、ドイツで学んだ森鷗外ら多くの文豪が、欧米の文学技法を取り入れた随筆、物語、小説を記した。欧米を手本にしてジャーナリズムも発展した。日本語の「新聞」（新しく聞くの意味）は、日本の近代化を推進した立役者の一人、福沢諭吉が編み出した単語である。ごく普通の日本人ですら欧米の風習に興味を抱いた時期であり、福沢のベストセラー（「学問のすゝめ」）がこの分野の教典となった。福沢諭吉は生涯を通じて、著作や翻訳を通じて教育のために大きく貢献し、日本初の私立大学である慶應義塾大学を創設した。

森鷗外
Ogai Mori

キリスト教は1873年に公式に認可され、欧米で学んだ多くの日本人キリスト者が世論形成に重要な役割を果たした。安部磯雄や片山潜のように、貧しい農民や労働者の苦境を目の当たりにして、キリスト教の教えを社会主義の綱領に当てはめた者もいた。社会的矛盾は、産業革命の成果と直接

福沢諭吉
Yukichi Fukuzawa

27. Cultural Movements in the Meiji Period

The Meiji Period marked the beginning of modern Japan. The country strove mightily to catch up with the standards of the more technologically and socially advanced Western nations. It invested heavily in the development of new educational, military, governmental, and administrative systems. By the end of the Meiji Period in 1912, Western influence could be seen in every corner of Japan, but particularly in the major cities, in everything from architecture to daily life. At the same time, an array of new cultural movements had also emerged.

This was most evident in literature and the arts. For example, the writers Soseki Natsume, who studied in London, and Ogai Mori, who studied in Germany, and many others penned essays, stories, and novels that incorporated Western literary techniques. Journalism also developed, following Western models. In fact, the Japanese word for newspaper—*shimbun* ("new hearings")—was created in the Meiji Period by Yukichi Fukuzawa, foremost among Japan's modernizers. This was a period in which even the average Japanese was intrigued by Western customs, and Fukuzawa's best-selling books were the authority on that subject. Throughout his life, Fukuzawa made huge contributions to the cause of education through his writings and translations, and eventually by founding Keio University, the first private university in Japan.

朝野新聞：民権派による
新聞の草分け (1874–93)
Choya Shimbun, an early activist newspaper (1874–93)

Christianity was officially sanctioned in 1873, and many Japanese Christians who had studied in the United States and Europe played important opinion-making roles. Some of them, like Isoo Abe and Sen Katayama,

の相関関係を示し、少数の富裕層が権力を握って大多数の貧困層を支配していた。社会主義者や共産主義者は強く抗議し、政府に弾圧された。

　欧米の影響が日本に及ぶと、反発が生まれるのもほぼ不可避であった。日本のアイデンティティを守るため、欧米の影響が浸透するのを憤り、ナショナリズム的感情を抱いた者も多かった。こうした感情はしばしば、国家神道と結びついていた。国家神道は、天皇の栄光の下に日本を統合しようとする計画の一環として明治政府が後押しした宗教である。神道と天皇の神性を結びつけようとする国粋主義的な傾向が、日本を第二次世界大戦へと駆り立てる上で一定の役割を演じることとなる。

applied their Christian beliefs to socialist causes after seeing the pathetic conditions of poor farmers and workers. Social contradictions showed a direct correlation to the accomplishments of the industrial revolution. The rich minority possessed the power and dominated the poor majority. Socialists and communists vigorously protested and were oppressed by the government in turn.

With so much Western influence coming into Japan, it was perhaps inevitable that a reaction should set in. In an effort to protect their Japanese identity, many people reacted to Western penetration with resentment and nationalistic sentiments. Such sentiments were often associated with state Shintoism, supported by the Meiji government as part of its plan to unite Japan under the emperor's glory. Nationalist inclinations linking Shintoism with the emperor's divinity eventually played a role in Japan's entry into World War II.

第6章 第二次世界大戦への道

28. 大正デモクラシー

　明治天皇が1912年に崩御し、明治時代は終わりを告げた。日本は多くの成功を遂げて国際的な地位も向上し、世界情勢における主要プレーヤーとなった。大正天皇が皇位を継承する頃には、日本人はその成果を実際に享受することができた。しかし第一次世界大戦の経済的損害は重大であり、政府はその解決策として増税に訴えた。この決断は大衆の抗議を招き、女権主義や共産主義などをはじめ大規模な社会運動を促した。その一方で、大正時代の特徴の一つに、民主主義的な空気があったことが挙げられる。政治的には、議会民主主義の動きが広がり、1925年にはついに、25歳以上の全ての男性に選挙権が与えられた。デモや政治集会も合法とされて頻繁に実施されたが、共産主義と社会主義は1925年に非合法化された。

　大正時代は全般的に民主主義的な空気が漂ったため、文化活動が活発化した。芥川龍之介、志賀直哉、谷崎潤一郎といった作家が近代日本文学の名作を生み出した。また、大正時代はマスメディアの揺籃期でもあった。1925年にラジオ放送が始まり、数々の雑誌や出版物が創刊された。

　しかし外交の面では、大正時代は軍部の発言権が増した時代であった。第一次世界大戦中、日本は英仏米とともに連合国側についた。主戦場はヨーロッパだったが、日本はこの機

Chapter 6:
Path to World War II

28. Taisho Democracy

The Meiji era ended with Emperor Meiji's death in 1912. Because of Japan's many successes, its international status had improved, and Japan had become a major player in world affairs. When Emperor Taisho succeeded to the throne, the Japanese were actually able to enjoy their achievements. The economic damage of World War I was serious, however, and the government's solution was to raise taxes. That decision moved the public to protest and encouraged widespread social movements, including feminism and communism. On the other hand, one of the distinctive features of the Taisho era was its democratic atmosphere. Politically, the movement for parliamentary democracy spread, and in 1925 suffrage was finally granted to all males above the age of twenty-five. Demonstrations and political gatherings were legalized and frequently held, though communism and socialism were banned in 1925.

The generally democratic mood of the Taisho era encouraged cultural activity. Writers like Ryunosuke Akutagawa, Naoya Shiga, and Junichiro Tanizaki created some of the most notable works in modern Japanese literature. Taisho also saw the dawn of mass media. Radio broadcasts started in 1925, and countless magazines and publications were launched.

In international relations, however, Taisho saw the Japanese military

第6章 第二次世界大戦への道

に中国での存在感を強めた。日本軍はドイツが支配していた山東半島を占領し、日本に政治、軍事的特権を付与するよう中国に迫った。中国では、中華民国が弱体化した清王朝に取って代わり、ナショナリズムが海外の帝国主義と戦う上での力となった。当然ながら、中国における日本の存在は反日感情を生んだ。

　明治末期から大正初期にかけて、日本は中国を視野に入れて、軍事力に多大な投資を始めた。日露戦争(1904-05)で日本がロシアを破ると、日本は西方、特に中国に影響力を拡大し始めた。これにより次第に、アメリカが日本最大の仮想敵国になった。1922年、アメリカの後押しにより、日、米、英、仏、伊は海軍の軍縮を目的としたワシントン条約を締結した。五か国はまた、太平洋と中国における権益を拡張する権利をそれぞれ有していることを確認した。

「黒船屋」：大正ロマン主義の中心人物の一人である竹久夢二の作

"Kurofuneya," by Yumeji Takehisa, a leading figure in the Taisho Romanticism movement

「赤玉ポートワイン」のポスター(1922)：最初のヌードポスター広告

A poster of "Akadama Port Wine," the first nude advertising poster in 1922

becoming more assertive. During World War I, Japan had joined the Allied powers along with England, France, and the United States. While the war was being fought mainly in Europe, Japan took the opportunity to expand its presence in China. The Japanese army occupied the German-controlled Shandong Peninsula and demanded that China grant Japan political and military privileges. In China itself, the weakened Qing Dynasty had given way to the Republic of China, and nationalism became a force in combating foreign imperialism. As a matter of course, the Japanese presence in China, gave rise to anti-Japanese sentiment.

It was around the end of Meiji and the beginning of Taisho that Japan began to invest heavily in its military machine, with China in its sights. After Japan defeated Russia in the Russo-Japanese War of 1904–1905, Japan set about expanding its influence westward, particularly to China. This led to the United States becoming Japan's greatest potential enemy. In 1922, at the urging of the United States, Japan, the U.S., England, France, and Italy signed the Washington Treaty to limit naval armaments. These nations also confirmed their own right to expand their interests in the Pacific and China.

旧東京駅：1914年12月20日開設
Old Tokyo Station, opened on December 20, 1914

29. 満州侵略

　第一次世界大戦が終わると世界経済は後退し、日本は厳しい不況に直面した。産業界はこの不況を乗り切る努力をしたが、二つの惨事により努力は水泡に帰した。まず1923年、東京は関東大震災に見舞われ、13万人以上が犠牲になった。これにより、経済が早期回復する可能性はなくなり、政府は大きな財政負担に苦しむこととなった。そして6年後の1929年、有名なウォール街の大暴落が起きた。大正天皇は1926年に崩御しており、昭和天皇（国外では諱の裕仁が知られている）の治世4年目の出来事であった。第一次世界大戦後の世界では、アメリカが世界最大の債権国になったため、金融恐慌の影響は日本を含む全ての国に及んだ。被害は広範囲に及び、銀行や重工業だけではなく、農業や小売業も大幅に後退した。農村では、貧困に陥った農民が娘を身売りし、息子たちは軍に入隊した。

　こうした厳しい時代を生き延びるため、財閥と呼ばれる日本の主要な金融産業連合体は、政府との結びつきを強めて、中国、特に満州で新たな市場や機会を見いだそうとした。三井、三菱、住友、安田、第一といった財閥は、主要政党

満州国の制服を着る皇帝溥儀
Emperor Puyi wearing a Manchukuo uniform

瀋陽市に入る日本の騎兵
Japanese cavalry entering Mukden (Shenyang)

29. Invasion of Manchuria

1923年の関東大震災後、シカゴで行われた「日本救済運動」

After 1923 Great Kanto earthquake, "Japan Relief Movement" was held in Chicago

When World War I came to an end, the world economy shrank, and Japan faced a serious recession. The efforts of Japanese industry to ride out this recession were nullified by two major catastrophes. In 1923, Tokyo was struck by a major earthquake that killed more than 130,000 people. This disaster destroyed any possibility of quick economic recovery and oppressed the government with a heavy financial burden. Six years later, the famous Wall Street crash of 1929 occurred. Emperor Taisho had passed away in 1926, and Japan was in the fourth year of the reign of Emperor Showa (known outside Japan as Hirohito). The United States had become the world's largest creditor nation in the post-World War I world, so the financial panic was felt in every country, including Japan. The damage was widespread. Not only banks and heavy industries but also agriculture and retailing were severely set back. In rural areas, impoverished farmers sold their daughters; their sons joined the army.

To survive these tumultuous times, Japan's major financial and industrial conglomerates, known as *zaibatsu*, strengthened their ties to government and decided to seek new markets and opportunities in China, particularly Manchuria. *Zaibatsu* such as Mitsui, Mitsubishi, Sumitomo, Yasuda, and, Daiichi had great influence on major political parties and gradually integrated with the military movement.

に大きな影響を与え、次第に軍部の動きと歩調を合わせていった。

1931年、日本軍は満州に対する攻勢を取った後に満州国という傀儡国家を創設し、清の元皇帝である溥儀を満州国の皇帝に据えた。これにより日本は国際社会の非難を浴びることとなった。国際連盟の主要加盟国はみな日本の領土拡張に反対したため、日本政府は国際連盟から脱退することを決めた。

第一次世界大戦は、世界の主要列強に多くの教訓をもたらした。列強は多大な代償を支払って、帝国主義は世界規模で修復不可能な損害をもたらしうることを学んだのである。しかし日本は平和や国際社会との共存の価値を認識しなかった。日本は、19世紀に開国を迫ったアメリカや他の欧米諸国に対して憤り続けており、狂信的なナショナリズムが見られるようになった。軍部、特に陸軍は傲慢な優越感を抱き、右翼の支援を得て世論を操作した。さまざまな社会運動が生じたが、非国民として抑圧された。

1932年、急進的な青年海軍将校が、議会与党の立憲政友会総裁であった犬養毅首相を暗殺した。1936年2月26日には、財閥と政府の蜜月関係に反発した青年将校がクーデターを起こし、元海軍将校の斎藤実（元）首相をはじめとする国会議員数人を殺害した。こうした騒動を経て、軍部は次第に中央政府の中で確固たる地位を占めるようになり、中国への侵略もさらに積極的な局面に突入した。その結果、大正時代に育まれた民主主義は完全に失われた。

In 1931, the Japanese army adopted a more aggressive stance in Manchuria and eventually created the puppet state of Manchukuo and installed the dethroned emperor Pu Yi of the Qing Dynasty as emperor. This resulted in Japan being condemned by the international community. Since all the major countries in the League of Nations were opposed to Japanese territorial expansion, the Japanese government decided to withdraw from the League.

World War I carried many lessons for the world's major powers. They had paid a tremendous price to learn that imperialism can cause irreparable damage on a worldwide scale. Japan itself failed to recognize the value of peace and co-existence in the world community. It remained resentful of the United States and other Western nations that had forced the country open in the nineteenth century, and a fanatic nationalism developed. The military, particularly the army, with its arrogant superiority complex, manipulated public opinion, with the support of the right wing. Various social movements were surpressed as unpatriotic.

In 1932, radical junior navy officers assassinated Tsuyoshi Inukai, the prime minister, who headed the Seiyu-kai, the majority party in the Diet. And on February 26, 1936, a group of young military officers, who were opposed to the close relationship between the *zaibatsu* and the government, launched a coup d'état and killed several Diet members, including Prime Minister Makoto Saito, a former naval officer. Amid the tumult, the military gradually assumed a dominant position in the central government, and the invasion of China took on a more aggressive dimension. In consequence, the democratic gains made in the Taisho era were completely swept away.

30. 中国との戦争

　日本軍が満州を掌握すると、反日感情が中国に広まった。この感情は強力であったため、毛沢東率いる共産主義者と、蒋介石の下で中国を公式に統治していた中国国民党との間で休戦協定が結ばれた。両者は1936年、抗日民族統一戦線を結成することで合意した。

　この同盟を打破するため、日本は1937年に大規模攻撃を仕掛け、北京近くの盧溝橋（マルコポーロ橋）で中国の駐屯部隊を圧倒した。日本は上海、南京（中華民国の首都）など多くの主要都市を占拠した。この時代に、日本は南京大虐殺を実施し、数十万人の中国人兵士や市民を殺害した。南京国民政府は南京から四川省の重慶へと逃れた。

　しかし、広大な中国領土における戦争の長期化により、日本軍は手薄になった。都市を占領することはできたが、山岳地帯や農村を支配することは不可能だったのである。また、日本軍の活動は、中国に大きな権益を有していたアメリカやイギリスとの深刻な緊張を招いた。両国は公式に中国を支援し、日本に経済制裁を行った。1939年、日本軍

日本の侵略の脅威に晒されて北京を後にする中国人兵士
Chinese soldiers leaving Beijing under threat of Japanese invasion

30. War Against China

After the Japanese army seized Manchuria, anti-Japanese sentiment spread in China. This sentiment was so strong that a truce was called between the Communists, under Mao Zedong, and the Nationalists, which officially governed China under the leadership of Chiang Kai-shek. The two sides agreed in 1936 to create a united front to resist the Japanese.

To crush this alliance Japan launched a massive attack in 1937, overwhelming a Chinese garrison at Lugou (Marco Polo) Bridge near Beijing. The Japanese occupied Shanghai, Nanjing (the Chinese capital), and many other major cities. It was during this time that the Japanese army committed atrocities in Nanjing, killing several hundred thousand Chinese soldiers and citizens. The Chinese government escaped from Nanjing to Chongqing in Sichuan.

However, long drawn-out battles in the vast Chinese territory stretched the Japanese army thin. They could occupy cities, but it was impossible to keep mountains and rural areas under their control. Also, the Japanese activities created serious tensions with the United States and England, which had considerable interests in China. They officially supported China and established economic sanctions against Japan. In Manchuria, the Japanese army attacked the Soviet Union in Nomonhan in 1939 over a territorial dispute. Stalin's army emerged victorious, and the two countries agreed thereafter to respect the borders of Mongolia and Manchukuo.

は領土問題のため、満州のノモンハンでソ連を攻撃した。スターリン軍が勝利し、両国はその後、モンゴルと満州の国境を尊重することで合意した。

この頃には日本は国際社会から孤立し、民主主義や平和に向けた国際的動向と反目していた。日本はまた、3世紀以上にわたり欧米がアジアで築いた財産を脅かす存在だとみなされた。

ドイツとイタリアも、ヨーロッパで同様の侵略を行っていた。1939年、ヨーロッパで第二次世界大戦が勃発した際には、ドイツは強大な戦力を誇っていた。最終的に、1940年に近衛文麿首相率いる内閣が締結した条約により、ドイツとイタリア、日本の三国は公式に同盟国となり、枢軸国が出現した。

経済制裁への対応や、中国との戦争を継続する必要に迫られた日本は、石油などの資源の安定供給を維持するべく東南アジアの侵略に着手した。日本軍は1941年にフランスの支配下にあるベトナムを侵略し、その結果アメリカは日本への石油の輸出を禁止する措置を取った。イギリスとオランダもすぐに追随した。

国内では、政府は国家的な危機を乗り切るために引き続き世論を操作し、全国民に団結を求めた。1938年、国家総動員法が通過し、政府は戦争を遂行するべく全てのメディア、産業、そして市民一人一人を統制することができるようになった。1940年、全政党が合体して大政翼賛会となった。その結果、国会は政府や軍部の決定に承認印を押すだけの存在にすぎなくなった。警察も憲兵も反政府運動を取り締まり、一般市民の日常生活に目を光らせ続けた。日本は事実上、軍事機構となった。

By now Japan was isolated from the international community and seen as inimical to movements for international democracy and peace. Japan was also seen as encroaching on Western assets created in Asia over more than three centuries.

Germany and Italy were making similarly aggressive efforts in Europe. When World War II broke out in Europe in 1939, Germany's strength was formidable. Finally, Germany, Italy, and Japan became official allies with a treaty signed in 1940 under the cabinet led by Prime Minister Fumimaro Konoe. Thus, the Axis powers came into being.

In response to the economic sanctions and the necessity of continuing the war against China, Japan proceeded to invade Southeast Asia to maintain stable supplies of oil and other resources. Japanese forces invaded French-controlled Vietnam in 1941, resulting in the U.S. decision to ban oil exports to Japan. England and the Netherlands quickly followed suit.

Domestically, the government continued to manipulate public opinion and call for all Japanese to unite to overcome this national crisis. In 1938, the State General Mobilization Law was passed, enabling government control over all media, industry, and individual citizens to prosecute the war effort. In 1940 all political parties were conflated into one, the Imperial Rule Assistance Association. As a result, the Diet became nothing more than a rubber stamp for government and military decisions. The police, both regular and military, clamped down on anti-government movements and kept a watchful eye on the daily lives of ordinary citizens. In effect, Japan had become a war machine.

31. 太平洋戦争と第二次世界大戦

　中国侵略や連合国との戦争に関する最終決定に昭和天皇がどの程度関与したかは定かではない。日本は明らかに強硬な軍部の指導下にあり、日本国民のみならず、政府や天皇その人をも軍部が操っていた。一方、近衛文麿首相のように、軍部の野心を抑えて、日本への禁輸措置を実施する国々に歩み寄ろうとした人物もいた。また米内光政元首相や山本五十六元帥のように、連合国との戦争に消極的な高官もいた。

　運命の日が近づいた1941年4月、日本は満州の北方国境の安定を目的とした中立条約をドイツに包囲されたソ連と締結した。次に、政府はアメリカに外交使節団を派遣し、緊張と経済制裁の緩和を試みた。ルーズベルト大統領とコーデル・ハル国務長官は、日本軍の中国からの完全撤退を要求した。しかし、交渉が行われている最中にも、帝国陸軍は文民政権の指示を頑なに無視して、中国や東南アジア全域にわたり戦線を拡大した。これにより英米とのさらなる緊張が生まれた。

フランクリン・D・ルーズベルト大統領
President Franklin D. Roosevelt

山本五十六
Isoroku Yamamoto

31. The Pacific War and World War II

The extent of Emperor Hirohito's involvement in making the final decision to invade China and wage war against the Allied nations remains a mystery. Japan was clearly under strong military leadership, which manipulated not only the Japanese public but the government and the emperor himself. On the other hand, there were men like Prime Minister Fumimaro Konoe, who wanted to tone down the military's ambitions and find a compromise with the nations embargoing Japan. There were also other high-ranking officials, such as former Prime Minister Mitsumasa Yonai and Admiral Isoroku Yamamoto, who were reluctant to go to war with the Allies.

As the fatal day approached, Japan signed a neutrality pact with the German-besieged Soviet Union in April of 1941 to secure the northern front in Manchuria. Second, the government sent diplomatic delegations to the United States to attempt to ease tensions and economic sanctions. President Roosevelt and his secretary of state, Cordell Hull, demanded full withdrawal of the Japanese army from China. However, even while the negotiations were being conducted, the Japanese army stubbornly ignored directions from the civilian government and expanded its war effort to areas throughout China and Southeast Asia. This increased tensions with the United States and England.

真珠湾フォード島横で沈む米海軍戦艦
U.S. Navy battleship sinking alongside Ford Island, Pearl Harbor

ついに1941年10月、陸軍大将の東条英機が首相となった。東条は英米との全面戦争を決断し、1941年12月7日（日本時間では12月8日）、海軍に真珠湾を攻撃させたのである。ハワイのアメリカ海軍は完全に不意を突かれて、7隻の戦艦と飛行機の約半数が破壊された。日本軍は同時にマレーシアとシンガポールを攻撃し、米軍基地があるフィリピンをはじめ、東南アジアの大部分を占領した。南太平洋諸島の多くも占領された。真珠湾攻撃から6か月もたたないうちに、日本軍はオーストラリア侵略の準備をしていた。

　日本の戦争推進プロパガンダは、大東亜共栄圏の標語に集約される。これは他のアジア諸国が立ち上がり、欧米帝国主義からの独立の達成を日本が支援するという意図であったが、日本国外では違う受け止め方をされていた。皮肉なことだが、日本が韓国併合や中国侵略を行わなければ、このプロパガンダは一定の共感を生んだかもしれない。しかし、現実は大東亜共栄圏のイデオロギーとはかけ離れていた。

32. 原子爆弾と日本の降伏

　日本の攻勢は初めの半年ほどは成功していたが、アメリカ海軍がミッドウェーの海戦で日本海軍に勝利したのがターニングポイントとなった。アメリカの経済力や軍事力は日本より堅固であり、戦争が長引くほど、日本の弱体化が明らかになった。

Finally, the army general Hideki Tojo became prime minister in October 1941. He decided on a full assault against the United States and England and had the Japanese navy and air force attack Pearl Harbor on December 7, 1941 (December 8 in Japan). The U.S. navy in Hawaii was taken completely by surprise—seven battleships and about half of the aircraft there were destroyed. Simultaneously, Japanese forces attacked Malaysia and Singapore and occupied most of Southeast Asia, including the Philippines, where a U.S. base was located. A number of South Pacific islands were also occupied. Within six months of Pearl Harbor, the Japanese army was making preparations to invade Australia.

Japanese pro-war propaganda was centered on the concept of a Greater East Asia Co-prosperity Sphere. This was intended to mean that Japan would help other Asian nations stand up to and achieve independence from Western imperialism, but it was perceived quite differently outside Japan. Ironically, if Japan had not annexed Korea and invaded China, this propaganda may have received some sympathy—but the reality was far removed from the ideology.

32. The Atomic Bomb and Surrender

Japan's offensive was successful for the first six months or so. Then the U.S. navy defeated the Japanese navy in the Battle of Midway. This became the turning point in the war. American economic and military power was more substantial than Japan's, and the longer the war continued, the more obvious Japan's weaknesses became.

第6章 第二次世界大戦への道

アメリカは南太平洋から反撃ののろしを上げ、日本軍を次第に北へと押し戻した。中国での日本陸軍は、果てしないゲリラ攻撃を防ぐために資源を使い果たしていた。東南アジアでは、イギリスが日本軍をビルマから撤退させた。1944年にサイパン島を奪取するとアメリカ空軍は日本本土に空襲をはじめ、太平洋でも次第に日本海軍を圧倒したが、これに対し、日本の航空隊は神風特別攻撃隊による自爆攻撃を行った。1945年4月には、アメリカ軍が沖縄に上陸を開始した。

ヨーロッパでは、イタリアは1943年に降伏し、連合国側はドイツを両側から攻撃していた。同年、ルーズベルト、チャーチル、蒋介石がカイロで会談を開き、戦後の取り決めについて話し合った。スターリンとルーズベルトは1945年2月にヤルタで再び会談し、ソ連が日本との中立条約を反故にして北方から満州を侵略することを確認した。ナチス・ドイツの崩壊後、連合国の首脳陣は1945年7月にポツダム宣言を発し、日本に無条件降伏を要求した。

ポツダム宣言は、軍国主義の撤廃、本州の占領、全ての海外領土の正当な権利者への返還などを定めていた。鈴木貫太郎首相が返答を渋っているうちに、原子爆弾が8月6日に広島、8月9日に長崎と計二発投下され、32万人を超える無辜の市民の命を奪った。ソ連も直ちに日本に宣戦布告し、満州を侵略した。

広島上空の原子雲
Atomic cloud over Hiroshima

Chapter 6: Path to World War II

Starting in the South Pacific, the United States began a counter-offensive, gradually pushing the Japanese back to the north. In China, the Japanese army was depleting its resources in fending off endless guerrilla attacks. In Southeast Asia, England pushed the Japanese back from Burma. After taking Saipan in 1944, the U.S. air force started a bombing campaign on Japan itself and in the Pacific gradually overcame the Japanese navy. In response, the Japanese air force resorted to suicidal *kamikaze* attacks. By April 1945, U.S. forces had begun landing on Okinawa.

In Europe, Italy had surrendered in 1943, and the Allied nations were attacking Germany from both sides. In the same year, Roosevelt, Churchill, and Chiang Kai-shek met in Cairo to discuss postwar arrangements. Stalin and Roosevelt met again in Yalta in February 1945 to confirm that the Soviet Union would invade Manchuria from the north, repudiating the neutrality pact with Japan. After the fall of Nazi Germany, the Allied leaders issued the Potsdam Declaration in July 1945, demanding that Japan surrender unconditionally.

The Potsdam Declaration included the elimination of militarism, the occupation of mainland Japan, and the return of all foreign territories to the appropriate claimants. While Prime Minister Kantaro Suzuki delayed his response, two atomic bombs were dropped—one on Hiroshima on August 6th, the other on Nagasaki on August 9th—killing more than 320,000 innocent civilians. The Soviet Union promptly declared war on Japan and invaded Manchuria.

降伏文書に署名する重光葵外務大臣
Foreign Minister Mamoru Shigemitsu
signs the Instrument of Surrender

8月14日、長引く議論の末に、政府はポツダム宣言の受諾を決定し、昭和天皇がラジオで全国民にその旨を告げた。9月2日、降伏した日本側が東京湾に停泊した米戦艦ミズーリ号上で降伏文書に公式に署名し、日本の軍部は解体した。

　その結果、朝鮮は独立し、台湾は中国に、南樺太はソ連に返還された。日本は310万人の人命を失い、国土と国民に計り知れない損害を被った。戦争からかなり時間が経っても、広島や長崎の被爆者が白血病で亡くなる例があった。中国では、無数の日本人の子供たちが戦後の混乱の中で親と離れ離れになり、その後二度と巡り会えない者も多かった。

　日本は侵略国家として近隣アジア諸国の信頼を完全に失った。現在でも、自衛隊の強化に神経をとがらせているアジアの国家は多い。日本にとっての重要課題は、日本が戦争を国家政策の道具として用いることを拒否し続けることを近隣諸国に納得させることであるが、この問題は近年再び表面化している。

　他方、アメリカとイギリスは勝者としての義務を負うことになった。軍国主義に反対して戦った立場としては、欧米の影響から逃れて独立したいというアジアの希望を拒絶することはできなかった。中国などのアジア諸国における巨大な権益と多くの特権をもたらした古い欧米の帝国主義が揺らぎ始め、第二次世界大戦、特に太平洋戦争が、アジアにおける帝国主義の終焉をもたらしたのである。

On August 14th, after prolonged argument and discussion, the government decided to accept the Potsdam Declaration, and Emperor Hirohito made an announcement to the nation over the radio. On September 2nd, the surrender was officially signed on the U.S. battleship Missouri in Tokyo Bay and the Japanese military dismantled.

As a result, Korea became independent, Taiwan was returned to China, and southern Sakhalin reverted to the Soviet Union. Japan had suffered the loss of 3.1 million lives and immeasurable damage to its land and people. Even long after the war, atomic bomb victims in Hiroshima and Nagasaki died from leukemia. In China, countless Japanese children were separated from their parents in the postwar chaos; many were never reunited.

Japan, as the aggressor nation, completely lost the trust of its Asian neighbors. Even now, many Asian countries are quite nervous about the development of the Japanese military. The essential challenge for Japan is to convince them that Japan will continue to reject the use of war as an instrument of national policy, an issue that recently has once again come to the fore.

On the other hand, the United States and England had obligations as winners. Having fought against militarism, they could not very well oppose Asian yearnings for independence from Western influence. The old Western imperialism, which had gained the West large interests and many privileges in China and other Asian nations, began to erode. World War II, particularly the Pacific war, brought an end to imperialism in Asia.

第7章 グローバル・パートナーシップの時代

33. 占領と改革

　日本の占領は、連合国軍最高司令官(SCAP)ダグラス・マッカーサー元帥の指導下に実施された。SCAPは、総司令部(GHQ)を通じて日本政府と連絡を取った。

　連合国の最初の仕事は、戦争犯罪者を訴追する裁判を開くことであった。極東国際軍事裁判が1946年5月に開廷され、東条英機元首相をはじめとする28名の軍人および政治指導者が、戦争を起こす共同謀議に参加したとして起訴された。より軽い罪で訴追された者も多くいた。同様の裁判が日本内外で開催され、全部で920人の被告が死刑判決を受けた。しかし、天皇は裁判にかけられず、投獄もされなかった。これは天皇が日本国民の統合において重要な役割を演じうるとSCAPが考えたからである。

　次に、SCAPは日本の民主国家化に乗り出した。戦争に協力した20万人強の公務員は公職追放となった。また、明治憲法は廃され、1947年5月に新憲法が施行された。新憲法の下では、天皇は神ではなく、国の象徴として新たに規定された。また第9条では、日本は国際紛争の解決手段として再び軍事力に訴えることはないと述べている。

昭和天皇とマッカーサー元帥
Emperor Hirohito and General MacArthur

Chapter 7:
The Era of Global Partnership

33. Occupation and Reform

The Occupation of Japan was carried out under the leadership of General Douglas MacArthur, who was appointed Supreme Commander of the Allied Powers (SCAP). SCAP communicated with the Japanese government through General Headquarters (GHQ).

The first task of the Allied Powers was to hold trials to prosecute war criminals. The International Military Tribunal for the Far East was convened in May 1946, and twenty-eight military and political leaders were charged with participating in a joint conspiracy to start and wage war, including former Prime Minister Hideki Tojo, among many others prosecuted for lesser crimes. Similar courts were held both inside and outside Japan, and 920 defendants in all were sentenced to death. The emperor, however, was neither tried nor sent to prison, because SCAP felt he could play an important role in unifying the Japanese public.

Next, SCAP set about making Japan a democratic nation. Over 200,000 bureaucrats who had cooperated in war activities were purged from public office. The old constitution was scrapped and a new one administered in May 1947. Under the new constitution, the emperor was redefined as the symbol of the nation instead of as a divinity. Also, Article IX stated that Japan would never again resort to military force as a means of settling international disputes.

第7章　グローバル・パートナーシップの時代

　新憲法は民主主義的な理念を反映して、資格を有する全国民に対し男女を問わず普通選挙権を認めるなど、議会制民主主義を規定した。さまざまな改革の一環として、言論、集会の自由や労働組合の活動といった民主主義の基本的な自由が保障された。財閥は日本によるアジア侵略における重要な要因であったため、GHQは財閥の解体を命じた。農地改革も実施され、小作農が自分の土地を所有できるようになった。

　戦争の影響は壊滅的であり、多くの人が家や仕事を失った。食料の供給も不足し、都市の住民の多くは飢えに苦しんだ。労働組合や言論の自由が保障されると、ストライキやデモが頻繁に行われるようになり、SCAPやGHQは共産主義の台頭をおそれるようになった。

　実際、世界の政治的状況はすでに冷戦時代へと急速に移行しつつあり、アメリカは日本を極東における民主主義国家の戦略的拠点に留めておくことを強く望んだ。

　したがって、アメリカの占領政策は次第に変化した。日本を民主主義、資本主義国家にするという目標を維持しつつも、アメリカは今や、ロシアや中国における共産主義レジームに対する緩衝材として、東アジアにおける開かれた市場を保護するために、日本が軍事力、経済力を備えた独立国家となることを望むようになった。

　この目標を達成するため、数人のアメリカの専門家が派遣されて、日本の税制や商制度の改正を支援した。同時に、日本の再軍備も始まった。新しい日本の軍隊は自衛隊と呼ばれるが、自衛隊が合憲か否かは今なお論争の対象となっている。

　こうした対日政策の方針転換に沿って、サンフランシスコ平和条約が連合国側の42か国とともに1951年に締結され

Reflecting democratic ideals, the new constitution provided for parliamentary democracy, including universal suffrage for all eligible citizens, both male and female. Among the many other reforms, basic democratic freedoms such as freedom of speech, assembly, and union activity were ensured. Since the *zaibatsu* were a major factor in the Japanese invasion of Asia, GHQ ordered them dismantled. The agricultural system was also reformed, with tenants now able to own their land.

The war was so devastating that myriads of people were bereft of homes and jobs. Food was in short supply and many urban citizens starved. With union activity and freedom of speech guaranteed, strikes and demonstrations were frequent occurrences, causing SCAP and GHQ to fear the rise of Communism.

In fact, the world political situation was already moving quickly toward the Cold War era, and the United States strongly favored keeping Japan at the strategic forefront of democratic countries in East Asia.

Accordingly, U.S. Occupation policy gradually shifted. While maintaining the goals of making Japan democratic and capitalist, the United States now favored an independent country with the military and economic power to serve as a buffer against the Communist regimes in Russia and China and protect open markets in East Asia.

To achieve that goal, several American specialists were dispatched to help implement changes in the Japanese tax and business systems. At the same time, Japan's rearmament was initiated. The new Japanese military was called the *Jieitai*, or Self-Defense Forces. Whether the Self-Defence Forces are constitutional is still a matter of dispute.

Based on this revised Japan policy, the San Francisco Peace Treaty was concluded in 1951 with forty-two allied nations. Simultaneously, the U.S.–Japan Mutual Security Treaty, was signed, with Japan approving U.S. military presence on its soil. In 1956 Japan applied to join the

た。同時に日米安全保障条約が締結され、日本は国内に米軍が駐在することを認めた。1956年、日本は国際連合に加盟を申請し、承認された。

　こうして沖縄と小笠原諸島を除き、占領は公式に終了した。米軍基地の多くが存在する沖縄では、完全な平和の達成と地域のニーズを充足する上でアメリカの存在が障害になるとしてしばしば抗議が行われている。小笠原諸島は1968年に日本に返還され、沖縄は1971年に日本の支配下に戻ってアメリカの占領状態から脱した。戦後はついに終わりを迎えたのである。

34. 高度経済成長とバブル経済

　第二次世界大戦で荒廃した日本は、独り立ちするために強力なリーダーシップを必要とした。はじめはマッカーサーがその必要を満たした。しかし、最終的に経済を活性化して前進させたのは、日本の政府と官僚だった。1868年の明治維新以来、官僚は常に日本の政府内で実権を握っていたのである。

　はじめは朝鮮戦争 (1950-53) によって始まった日本経済の復興は、1960年代に加速した。池田勇人首相が10年以内に日本人の所得を倍増すると公約してから、経済はロケットのように離陸し、年間GDP成長率は10%を超えた。一人あたり所得については、1960年代に三倍にも増加している。この驚異的な経済復興を象徴する出

池田勇人首相
Prime Minister Hayato Ikeda

United Nations and was approved.

Thus, the Occupation officially ended, except for Okinawa and the Ogasawara Islands. In Okinawa, where most of the U.S. military bases are located, there have been occasional protests against the American presence as an obstacle to achieving a full peace and fulfilling local needs. The Ogasawara chain was returned to Japan in 1968, and Okinawa's occupation status ended in 1971 when it reverted to Japanese control. The postwar era had finally come to an end.

34. Era of High Economic Growth and the Bubble Economy

Devastated by World War II, Japan needed strong leadership to get back on its feet. Initially, MacArthur filled that need. However, it was the Japanese government and bureaucracy who eventually galvanized the economy and drove it forward. Since the Meiji Restoration in 1868, bureaucrats had always been the real power holders in the Japanese government.

Japan's economic recovery, triggered initially by the Korean War (1950–53), gained speed in the 1960s. After Prime Minister Hayato Ikeda promised that Japanese income would double within a decade, the economy took off like a rocket and the annual GDP growth rate exceeded 10%. Per capita income actually tripled in the 1960s. The symbolic events representing this amazing economic recovery were the Tokyo Olympic Games in 1964—the first Olympics held in Asia—and

第7章　グローバル・パートナーシップの時代

来事は、アジアではじめて開催されたオリンピックである1964年の東京オリンピックや、同年の新幹線開通が挙げられる。

しかしこうした高度経済の代償として公害が深刻化し、商品や不動産の価格も大幅に上昇した。

生活水準は経済成長に比例しなかった。住宅水準の向上は今日でも、特に日本の大都市ではきわめて深刻な課題である。

経済の成功により日本は自信を次第に取り戻し、1970年代には、新生日本は国際情勢に関わりを深めていった。1980年代には、日本は世界第二位の経済大国になり、経済援助の面では世界第一位となった。反面、主要欧米貿易相手国は不公正な貿易慣行により日本が貿易黒字を享受しているとして、日本を非難した。

経済的成功が長年続くと、日本が今なお強固な官僚制度を必要としているかどうかが問題となる。貿易規制の問題については、戦後の荒廃から日本経済の舵取りをするために規制が必要であったのは事実である。しかし、世界が市場のグローバル化の時代に突入すると、古い規制の多くは時代遅れになった。それでも官僚は政策の変更に抵抗した。自らの権力や威信を損なうことになるからである。一方、内外からの規制緩和に向けた圧力は強まった。

実際に、日本はグローバルパートナーとしての責任の一端を担うよう求められている。この点については、国内でも熱い公開討論の対象となっている。中曽根康弘首相（在任1982-1987）の時代から、世界の不安定な地域における国連平和維持部隊に対し何らかの軍事的援助を

東京オリンピック開会式
（1964年）
Tokyo Olympics 1964
Opening Ceremony

the inauguration in the same year of the Shinkansen, the famous Bullet Train.

But this rapid growth exacted a price, with escalating pollution and vast increases in the cost of goods and real estate. The standard of living simply could not keep pace. Improvement in housing standards remains one of Japan's most serious problems, particularly in big cities.

Economic success gradually restored Japanese confidence, and by the 1970s renewed Japan became increasingly involved in international affairs. In the 1980s Japan became the world's number two economic power and number one in foreign aid. On the debit side, key Western trading partners frequently accused Japan of enjoying a trade surplus because of unfair trading practices.

Now, after years of economic success, it is questionable whether Japan still needs such a strongly entrenched bureaucracy. On the issue of trade regulations, regulations were necessary to steer the Japanese economy through the devastation following the war. However, once the world entered the era of market globalization, many of the old regulations became outdated. But bureaucrats have resisted policy change, because that would mean a reduction of their power and prestige. In the meanwhile, both domestic and international pressure for deregulation has intensified.

In fact, Japan has been urged to share the responsibility of being a global partner. This has been a hot item of public discussion in Japan. Since the time of Prime Minister Yasuhiro Nakasone (served 1982–87), one of the most important public issues has been whether Japan should give any kind of military aid to the U.N. peace-keeping forces in the world's unstable areas. In a partial resolution to this issue, in 1992 the Diet passed a law that permitted the Self-Defense Forces to participate in U.N. medical, refugee repatriation, logistical support, infrastructural

すべきか否かが日本の公共問題における最大の問題の一つとなっている。この問題を部分的に解決するため、国会は1992年に、自衛隊が国連の医療、難民の帰還、物資支援、インフラ再建、選挙監視および警察活動について厳格な制限の下で参加することを認める法律を制定した。安倍晋三政権下において、自衛隊の役割のさらなる拡大が検討されている。

　1980年末までの日本経済の強力な成長は、「バブル経済」という言葉を生み出した。不動産の価値は急騰し、巨額な利益を手にした金融機関は実業界に投資の拡大を促した。そして日本企業は事務所や工場を世界中に建設した。

　残念ながら、経済の拡大は腐敗を招き、政治家や官僚への不信感を生んだ。不動産価値の下落により1991年にバブルが弾けると、日本経済は1990年代全体にわたる不況に突入した。政府や官僚に対する国民の信頼度も、経済とともに下降線をたどった。

　2012年に自民党が再び政権に返り咲き、安倍晋三総理の下で、政府支出の拡大と前例のない金融緩和によるデフレ対策と日本経済再活性化の試みがなされている。この取り組みの長期的な成果についてはまだ未知数である。

reconstruction, election-monitoring, and policing operations under strictly limited conditions. Further expansion of the role of the Self-Defence Forces is now under consideration by the Shinzo Abe administration.

By the late 1980s, the strong growth of the Japanese economy spawned the term "bubble economy." The value of real estate escalated precipitously; financial institutions benefitted hugely and encouraged industry to wider investment; Japanese businesses expanded their offices and factories worldwide.

Unfortunately, economic inflation led to corruption and fostered feelings of distrust toward politicians and bureaucrats. When the bubble burst in 1991 owing to the devaluation of real estate, the economy slid into a recession that lasted throughout the 1990s. The public's approval rating of the government and bureaucracy went downhill along with the economy.

With the return to power of the Liberal Democratic Party's Shinzo Abe as prime minister in 2012, an attempt is being made to defeat deflation and reinvigorate the Japanese economy through increased government spending and unprecedented money easing. The long-term results of this effort are yet to be seen.

35. 今後の見通し

　1990年代は、日本にとってのターニングポイントであったと言える。バブル崩壊がもたらした厳しい時代は、経済のみならず社会にも影響を与えて、日本は社会の伝統的な価値観や慣わしの多くを変更する必要に迫られた。金融機関が弱体化し、大企業も新しいグローバルな競争に首尾よく参画するために根本的な内部調整を必要としたが、企業と政府官僚との間に根付いた人的制度や人的な結びつきは、今なお残っている。その結果、勝者と敗者が生まれた。変化に失敗した企業、あるいは変化を拒んだ企業は衰退し、倒産した。外資系企業は規制緩和の新興と不動産価値の下落を利用して日本市場に投資した。こうして日本は、経済的多様性の時代に突入した。

　世代の変化も生じつつある。バブル経済期に成長した若い世代は、日本の経済機構を作り上げたと考えられている「会社に全てを捧げる」という精神ではなく、私生活や余暇を重視するようになった。

　こうした価値観の変化により、個性を尊重し、日本の若者を世界で通用する人材に育てるような教育制度に向けた改革にかんする新たな論争が生じた。

　日本の長い歴史に鑑みても、いや、明治時代の改革と比べても、これらは容易な問題ではない。アジアの一員としての日本は、グローバルな変化を伝統的なアジア的価値観に統合するという課題を抱えており、この問題の解決はさらに困難である。

　第二次世界大戦を通じて、日本は東洋と西洋の文化の相乗関係を無視することがいかに危険であるかを学んだ。こうした相反する価値観が生み出した特異点として、ファシ

35. Predictions for the Future

The decade of the 1990s may be seen as a turning point for Japan. The tough times brought about by the bubble bursting have had not only economic repercussions but social ones as well, causing Japan to face the necessity of change in many of its traditional social values and practices.

Although weakened financial institutions and big industry needed drastic internal change to participate successfully in the new global competition, the entrenched human resource systems and relationships between business and government bureaucrats have remained in place.

As a result, winners and losers emerged. Companies that could not or would not change have declined or gone bankrupt. Foreign institutions took advantage of the increasing deregulation and the devaluation of real estate to invest in the Japanese market. Japan has thus entered an era of economic diversity.

A change of generations is also taking place. The younger generations that grew up during the economic bubble have begun to put more value on their private lives and leisure time than on the "everything for the company" mentality, commonly believed to have created the Japanese economic juggernaut.

This kind of value shift also brought on a new controversy about reforming the Japanese educational system to foster greater respect for individuality and to prepare Japanese young people to function globally.

Considering Japan's long history, even including the Meiji era reforms, these are not easy challenges. Indeed, for Japan as an Asian country, they are made all the more difficult by the question of how to incorporate globalizing changes into traditional Asian values.

In the cauldron of World War II, Japan learned the fatal risks of ignoring the synergistic relations between Eastern and Western cultures.

ズムや軍国主義が日本人の心に育まれたのである。しかし
今や、世界はかつての世界とは違う。多様化し、グローバ
ル化が進んでいるのである。日本がこの問題に取り組まな
ければならないことは確かだが、どのように取り組むかが、
今後の課題である。

Fascism and militarism developed as a result of the anomaly between such opposing values in the Japanese mind. Now, however, the world is different. It is becoming more and more diverse, more and more globalized. Japan will have to rise to this challenge, but just how it will do it is a question for the future.

TIME LINE

12,000 B.C. Jomon Period

Jomon culture / Jomon pottery

300 B.C. Yayoi Period

Yayoi culture / irrigated rice cultivation

A.D. 57	The Na state of Wa (Japan) sends envoy to the Later Han
239	Himiko of the Yamatai kingdom sends envoy to the Wei Dynasty

A.D. 300 Yamato Period

ca. 350	Yamato dynasty established
538	Arrival of Buddhism
587	Soga Clan defeats Mononobe Clan
593	Prince Shotoku becomes regent to Empress Suiko
604	Seventeen-article constitution promulgated
645	Taika Reform
701	Taiho Constitution

710 Nara Period

710	Imperial court moves to Nara (Heijo)
712	Kojiki (Records of Ancient Matters)
720	Nihonshoki (The Chronicles of Japan)
ca. 759	Man'yoshu (Collection of Myriad Leaves)
784	Imperial court moves to Nagaoka

794 Heian Period

794	Imperial court moves to Heian
800-	Tang culture widely adopted
	Saicho and Kukai return from China and found two new Buddhist sects
	Hiragana and katakana created
ca. 1008	The Tale of Genji
1016	Fujiwara clan at the height of its power
1156	Hogen War
1159-85	Gempei War
1167	Taira no Kiyomori appointed grand minister
1185	Fall of the Heike

1185 Kamakura Period

1192	Minamoto no Yoritomo appointed shogun
1221	New Pure Land Buddhist sects established
1274	First Mongol invasion (Battle of Bun'ei)
1281	Second Mongol invasion (Battle of Koan)

1333 Muromachi (Ashikaga) Period

1333	Fall of the Kamakura shogunate
1334	Kemmu Restoration
1336	Emperor Godaigo reigns at the court of Yoshino
	Era of Northern and Southern Courts begins
1338	Ashikaga Takauji appointed shogun
1368	Ashikaga Yoshimitsu becomes third shogun
1392	Yoshimitsu consolidates the shogunate
1467-77	Onin War (beginning of Warring States Period)
1543	Portuguese ship makes landfall on Tanegashima
1549	Christianity introduced to Japan by Jesuit missionary Francis Xavier

1568 Azuchi-Momoyama Period

1568	Oda Nobunaga enters Kyoto
1573	End of Muromachi (Ashikaga) shogunate
1582	Honno-ji Incident (death of Oda Nobunaga)
1590	Toyotomi Hideyoshi completes unification of the country
1592	Hideyoshi's first invasion of Korea (Bunroku no eki)
1597	Hideyoshi's second invasion of Korea (Keicho no eki)

1600 Edo Period

1600	Battle of Sekigahara
1603	Tokugawa Ieyasu establishes Tokugawa shogunate
1615	Fall of Toyotomi clan
1637	Shimabara Rebellion
1641	The shogunate completes seclusion policy
1688-	The Genroku era
	Bunraku puppet theater and haiku flourish
1782-	Great Tenmei Famine
1804-	The Bunka-Bunsei era
	Ukiyo-e and Kabuki flourish
1832-	Great Tempo Famine
1853	Commodore Matthew Perry arrives in Uraga Bay
1854	The Treaty of Kanagawa. The end of Japan's isolation policy
1867	Tokugawa Yoshinobu, the last shogun, resigns

1868 Meiji Period

1868	Meiji Restoration
1868	Boshin War
1877	Seinan War

1885	Cabinet system adopted with Hirobumi Ito as the first prime minister
1894	First Sino-Japanese War
1895	Peace Treaty of Shimonoseki
1902	Anglo-Japanese Alliance
1904	Russo-Japanese War
1905	Peace Treaty of Portsmouth
1910	Japan annexes Korea

1912 Taisho Period

1912	Death of Emperor Meiji
1914	World War I
1919	March First Movement
1922	Washington Naval Treaty
	Magazine/book publication flourishes
	Suffrage granted to all males above 25
	Radio broadcasting begins

1926 Showa Period

1926	Death of Emperor Taisho
1929	Wall Street Crash
1931	Manchurian (Mukden) Incident
1932	Puppet state of Manchukuo established
1936	February 26 Incident
1937	Marco Polo (Lugou) Bridge Incident, setting off second Sino-Japanese War
1939	Nomonhan (Khalkhin Gol) Incident
1940	Tripartite Pact among Japan, Germany, and Italy
1941	Pacific War starts with Japan's attack on Pearl Harbor
1945	United States drops atomic bombs on Hiroshima and Nagasaki. Japan surrenders
1947	New Japanese constitution promulgated
1951	San Francisco Peace Treaty signed
1964	Olympic Games held in Tokyo

1989 Heisei Period

1989	Death of Emperor Showa
1990s	Economic bubble bursts
1995	Great Hanshin Earthquake
	Tokyo subway sarin gas attack
2001	September 11 terrorist attacks on the U.S.
2003	Iraq war
2011	Great East Japan Earthquake and Tsunami
2012	Shinzo Abe becomes prime minister and introduces easy money policies

INDEX

A

Akechi Mitsuhide, *67*
Alessandro Valignano, *63*
Alexander the Great, *21*
Amida (Amitābha), *43*
anti-Japanese sentiment, *119*
Article IX, *138*
Ashikaga clan, *51*
Ashikaga shogunate, *51*
Ashikaga Takauji, *51*
Ashikaga Yoshiaki, *65*
Ashikaga Yoshimasa, *57*
Asuka Period, *23*
Atomic Bomb, *131*
Axis powers, *127*
Azuchi Castle, *67*
Azuchi-Momoyama, *71*

B

Balhae (Bokkai), *29*
Battle of Midway, *131*
Battle of Sekigahara, *73*
black-hulled ships, *83*
Boshin War, *97*
bubble economy, *141*
Buddhism, *21*
Bunka-Bunsei era, *87*
Bunraku puppet theater, *85*
bushi, *37*
Bushido (the code of the warrior), *41*

C

Chang'an, *27, 29*
Chiang Kai-shek, *125, 133*
Chikamatsu Monzaemon, *87*
Choshu, *95*
Churchill, *133*
Cold War era, *139*
Commodore Matthew Perry, *83, 93*
Communism, *117*
Confucianism, *79*
Cordell Hull, *129*

D

Daitoku-ji, *45, 55*
Date, *61, 83*

Dejima, *81*
Douglas MacArthur, *137*

E

Edo Castle, *79*
Emperor Godaigo, *49*
Emperor Kammu, *29*
Emperor Komei, *97*
Emperor Meiji, *97*
Emperor Nintoku, *19*
Emperor Shomu, *27*
Emperor Showa, *121*
Emperor Taisho, *117*
Emperor Tenji, *23*
Empress Gemmei, *27*
Empress Suiko, *23*
Engaku-ji, *45*

F

Francis Xavier, *63*
Fujiwara clan, *35*
Fumimaro Konoe, *127, 129*

G

Gempei War, *39*
General Headquarters (GHQ), *137*
Genji, *39*
Genji Monogatari (The Tale of Genji), *33*
Genroku era, *87*
Ginkaku-ji (the Temple of the Silver Pavilion), *57*
Greater East Asia Co-prosperity, *131*

H

haiku, *87*
han, *79, 89*
Hayato Ikeda, *141*
Heian Period, *29*
Heian-kyo, *29*
Heike, *39*
Heike Monogatari (The Tale of Heike), *39*
Hideki Tojo, *131, 137*
Hideyori, *73*
Himiko, *15*
hiragana, *35*
Hirobumi Ito, *103, 109*
Hirohito, *121*

Hiroshima, *133*
Hojo, *61*
Hojo clan, *39*
Hoke-kyo (Lotus Sutra), *43*
Honen, *43*
Honno-ji, *67*
Horyu-ji temple, *23*

I

Imperial Rule Assistance Association, *127*
International Military Tribunal for the Far East, *137*
Ise Shrine, *31*
Ishida Mitsunari, *73*
Isoo Abe, *113*
Isoroku Yamamoto, *129*

J

James Clavell, *75*
Jieitai, *139*
Jodo Shinshu (the New Pure Land Sect), *43*
Jodo-kyo, *43*
Jodo-shu (the Pure Land Sect), *43*
Jomon Period, *11*
Junichiro Tanizaki, *117*

K

Kabuki, *85*
Kamakura Period, *43*
kami, *31*
kamikaze, *49*
kamikaze attacks, *133*
Kan'ami, *57*
kanji, *19*
Kano school, *71*
Kantaro Suzuki, *133*
Kanzo Uchimura, *109*
katakana, *35*
Katsushika Hokusai, *85*
Kemmu Restoration, *51*
Kencho-ji, *45*
Kenzuishi, *23*
Kinkaku-ji (the Temple of the Golden Pavilion), *55*
Kitabatake Chikafusa, *53*
Kitagawa Utamaro, *85*
Kitayama, *55*
kofun, *19*
Koguryo (Kokuri), *17*
Kojiki (Records of Ancient Matters), *29*

Korean War, *141*
Kublai Khan, *47*
Kukai, *31*

L

Lady Murasaki, *31*
League of Nations, *123*

M

Makoto Saito, *123*
Manchuria, *121*
Man'yoshu (Collection of Myriad Leaves), *29*
Mao Zedong, *125*
March First Movement, *111*
Marco Polo, *25, 49*
Masatake Terauchi, *111*
Matsuo Basho, *87*
Meiji Constitution, *101*
Meiji government, *95*
Meiji Restoration, *97*
Minamoto no Sanetomo, *39*
Minamoto no Yoritomo, *39*
Ming Dynasty, *61*
Mitsumasa Yonai, *129*
Mongolian Invasion, *47*
Mononobe clan, *23*
Mori, *61*
Muromachi shogunate, *51*
Myoshin-ji, *55*

N

Nagaoka, *29*
Nagasaki, *133*
Nakatomi no Kamatari, *23*
Nanjing, *125*
Nanzen-ji, *45, 55*
Naoya Shiga, *117*
Nara Period, *25*
Nazi Germany, *133*
nembutsu chant, *43*
Neo-Confucianism, *79*
Nichiren, *43*
Nichiren-shu, *43*
Nihonshoki (The Chronicles of Japan), *29*
Nomonhan, *125*

O

Occupation, *137*
Oda Nobunaga, *65*
Ogai Mori, *113*
Onin War, *57*

Osaka Castle, *71*
Ottoman Empire, *61*

P

Pacific War, *129*
Paekche (Kudara), *17*
Pax Tokugawa, *87*
Pearl Harbor, *131*
Portsmouth, *109*
Potsdam Declaration, *133*
Prince Nakano-oe (Nakano-oe no Oji), *23*
Prince Shotoku, *23*
Protestant Reformation, *61*
Pu Yi, *123*

Q

Qin Dynasty, *13*
Qing Dynasty, *105*

R

Republic of China, *119*
Reunification, *65*
ronin, *91*
Roosevelt, *129*, *133*
Russo-Japanese War, *105*
Ryoan-ji, *45*
Ryunosuke Akutagawa, *117*

S

Saicho, *31*
Sakai, *59*
Sakamoto Ryoma, *95*
samurai, *37*
San Francisco Peace Treaty, *139*
sankin kotai, *89*
Saracen Empire, *25*
Satsuma, *89*, *95*
Seinan War, *101*
Seiyu-kai, *123*
Self-Defense Forces, *139*
Sen Katayama, *113*
Sen no Rikyu, *71*
Shilla (Shiragi), *19*
Shimabara, *83*
Shimazu, *61*
Shingon, *31*
Shinkansen, *143*
Shinran, *43*
Shinto, *31*
Shintoism, *29*, *33*
Shinzo Abe, *145*

Shōgun (novel), *75*
shogun, *39*
Shoso-in, *27*
Shusui Kotoku, *109*
Siddhartha Gautama, *21*
Silk Road, *25*
Soga clan, *23*
Soga no Iruka, *23*
Song Dynasty, *33*, *45*
Soseki Natsume, *113*
South Manchuria Railway, *109*
Southern and Northern Courts era, *51*
Southern Court, *51*
Soviet Union, *125*
Stalin, *133*
State General Mobilization Law, *127*
Sui Dynasty, *23*
Supreme Commander of the Allied Powers
  (SCAP), *137*
Suzuki Harunobu, *85*

T

Taiho Constitution, *25*
Taika Reform, *23*
Taira no Kiyomori, *39*
Taisho Democracy, *117*
Taisho era, *117*
Takamori Saigo, *95*, *101*
Takayoshi Kido, *99*
Takeda, *61*
Tale of Genji (Genji Monogatari), *33*
Tanegashima, *63*
Tang Dynasty, *25*
Tendai, *31*
Tenryu-ji, *55*
The Meiji Period, *97*
Theodore Roosevelt, *109*
Todai-ji temple, *27*
Tofuku-ji, *55*
Tokugawa feudal system, *89*
Tokugawa Ieyasu, *67*
Tokugawa Shogunate, *73*
Tokugawa Yoshinobu, *95*
Tokyo Olympic Games, *141*
Tomomi Iwakura, *99*
Tosa, *95*
Toshimichi Okubo, *99*
Toshusai Sharaku, *85*

Toyotomi Hideyoshi, *69*
Treaty of Shimonoseki, *105*
Tsunayoshi, *87*
Tsuyoshi Inukai, *123*

U

Uesugi, *61*
Ukiyo-e, *85*
United Nations, *141*

W

Wall Street crash of 1929, *121*
warlords, *61*
Warring States Period, *57*
Washington Treaty, *119*
Wei Dynasty, *15*
Wokou (Wako), *63*
World War II, *117, 129*

Y

Yakushi-ji temple, *25*
Yalta, *133*
Yamana clan, *53*
Yamatai kingdom, *15*
Yamato clan, *15*
Yamato Imperial Court, *17*
Yasuhiro Nakasone, *143*
Yayoi Period, *11*
Yoshimitsu, *53*
Yuan Dynasty, *47*
Yukichi Fukuzawa, *113*

Z

zaibatsu, *121*
Zeami, *57*
Zen, *45, 55*

あ

芥川龍之介 *116*
明智光秀 *66*
足利氏 *50*
足利尊氏 *50*
足利幕府 *50*
足利義昭 *64*
足利義政 *56*
足利義満 *52*
飛鳥時代 *22*
安土城 *66*
安土桃山時代 *70*
安部磯雄 *112*
安倍晋三 *144*
阿弥陀 *42*
アレキサンダー大王 *20*
アレッサンドロ・ヴァリニャーノ *64*
池田勇人 *140*
石田三成 *72*
イスラム帝国 *24*
伊勢神宮 *30*
伊藤博文 *102, 108*
犬養毅 *122*
岩倉具視 *98*
上杉氏 *60*
ウォール街の大暴落 *120*
浮世絵 *84*
内村鑑三 *108*
江戸城 *76*
円覚寺 *44*
応仁の乱 *56*
大久保利通 *98*
大坂城 *68*
オスマン帝国 *60*
織田信長 *64*

か

片仮名 *34*
片山潜 *112*
葛飾北斎 *84*
狩野派 *70*
歌舞伎 *84*
鎌倉時代 *42*
神 *30*
神風 *48*
神風特別攻撃隊 *132*

観阿弥 *56*
漢字 *18*
桓武天皇 *28*
魏 *14*
喜多川歌麿 *84*
北畠親房 *52*
北山 *54*
木戸孝允 *98*
共産主義 *116*
極東国際軍事裁判 *136*
金閣寺 *54*
銀閣寺 *56*
空海 *30*
百済国 *16*
黒船 *82*
元寇 *46*
源氏 *38*
原子爆弾 *130*
源氏物語 *32*
遣隋使 *22*
元朝 *46*
建長寺 *44*
源平合戦 *38*
建武の新政 *50*
元明天皇 *26*
元禄時代 *84*
高句麗国 *16*
幸徳秋水 *108*
孝明天皇 *96*
ゴータマ・シッダールタ *20*
コーデル・ハル *128*
国際連合 *140*
国際連盟 *122*
古事記 *28*
後醍醐天皇 *48*
国家総動員法 *126*
近衛文麿 *126, 128*
古墳 *18*

さ

西郷隆盛 *94, 100*
最澄 *30*
斎藤実 *122*
財閥 *120*
堺 *58*
坂本龍馬 *94*

薩摩藩 *88, 94*
侍 *36*
三・一運動 *110*
参勤交代 *88*
サンフランシスコ平和条約 *138*
GHQ *136*
自衛隊 *138*
ジェームズ・クラベル *74*
志賀直哉 *116*
島津氏 *60*
島原(の乱) *82*
宗教改革 *60*
儒教 *78*
蒋介石 *124, 132*
Shōgun(小説) *74*
正倉院 *26*
浄土教 *43*
聖徳太子 *22*
浄土宗 *43*
浄土真宗 *42*
聖武天皇 *26*
縄文時代 *10*
昭和天皇 *120*
新羅 *18*
シルクロード *24*
清王朝 *104*
新幹線 *142*
真言宗 *30*
新儒学 *78*
真珠湾 *130*
清朝 *12*
神道 *30*
親鸞 *42*
隋 *22*
推古天皇 *22*
枢軸国 *126*
鈴木貫太郎 *432*
鈴木春信 *84*
スターリン *132*
世阿弥 *56*
征夷大将軍 *38*
西南戦争 *100*
セオドア・ルーズベルト *108*
関ヶ原の戦い *72*
戦国時代 *56*

157

戦国大名 60
禅宗 44
禅寺 54
千利休 70
占領 136
宋 32, 44
蘇我氏 22
蘇我入鹿 22
ソ連 126

た
大化の改新 22
(日本憲法)第9条 136
大正時代 116
大正デモクラシー 116
大正天皇 116
大政翼賛会 126
大東亜共栄圏 130
大徳寺 44, 54
第二次世界大戦 116, 128
太平洋戦争 128
大宝律令 24
平清盛 38
ダグラス・マッカーサー 136
武田氏 60
伊達氏 60, 82
谷崎潤一郎 116
種子島 62
近松門左衛門 86
チャーチル 132
中華民国 118
長安 26, 28
長州藩 94
朝鮮戦争 140
出島 80
寺内正毅 110
天下統一 66
天智天皇 22
天台宗 30
天龍寺 54
唐 24
東京オリンピック 142
東洲斎写楽 84
東条英機 130, 136
東大寺 26
東福寺 54

徳川家康 66
徳川綱吉 84
徳川幕府 72
徳川慶喜 94
土佐 94
豊臣秀吉 68

な
長岡京 28
長崎 132
中曽根康弘 142
中臣鎌足 22
中大兄皇子 22
ナチス・ドイツ 132
夏目漱石 112
奈良時代 24
南京 124
南禅寺 44, 54
南朝 50
南北朝時代 50
日蓮 42
日蓮宗 42
日露戦争 104
日本書紀 28
仁徳天皇 18
念仏 42
ノモンハン 126

は
俳句 86
バブル経済 140
藩 78, 88
反日感情 118
秀頼 72
卑弥呼 14
平仮名 34
広島 132
裕仁 120
溥儀 122
福沢諭吉 112
武士 36
武士道 40
藤原氏 34
仏教 20
フビライ・ハン 46
フランシスコ・ザビエル 62
文化・文政期 76

文楽 84
平安京 28
平安時代 28
平家 38
平家物語 38
封建制度 88
北条氏 38, 60
法然 42
法隆寺 22
ポーツマス 108
法華経 42
戊辰戦争 96
渤海 28
ポツダム宣言 132
本能寺 66

ま
マシュー・ペリー司令官 82, 92
松尾芭蕉 86
マルコ・ポーロ 24, 48
満州 120
万葉集 28
ミッドウェーの海戦 130
南満州鉄道 108
源実朝 38
源頼朝 38
妙心寺 54
明朝 62
紫式部 34
室町幕府 50
明治維新 96
明治憲法 100
明治時代 96
明治政府 94
明治天皇 96
毛沢東 124
毛利氏 60
物部氏 22
森鷗外 112

や
薬師寺 24
邪馬台国 14
大和朝廷 16
大和民族 14
山名氏 52
山本五十六 128

弥生時代　*10*
ヤルタ　*132*
米内光政　*128*

ら
立憲政友会　*122*
龍安寺　*44*
ルーズベルト　*128, 133*
冷戦時代　*138*
連合国軍最高司令官　*136*
浪人　*90*

わ
倭寇　*62*
ワシントン条約　*118*

- E-CATとは…

英語が話せるようになるためのテストです。インターネットベースで、30分であなたの発話力をチェックします。

www.ecatexam.com

- iTEP®とは…

世界各国の企業、政府機関、アメリカの大学300校以上が、英語能力判定テストとして採用。オンラインによる90分のテストで文法、リーディング、リスニング、ライティング、スピーキングの5技能をスコア化。iTEP®は、留学、就職、海外赴任などに必要な、世界に通用する英語力を総合的に評価する画期的なテストです。

www.itepexamjapan.com

対訳 日本小史
JAPAN: A SHORT HISTORY

2018年3月10日 第1刷発行

著　　者　西海コエン
監 修 者　ジョン・ギレスピー
英文リライト　マイケル・ブレーズ
日本語訳　平　湊音
発 行 者　浦　晋亮
発 行 所　IBCパブリッシング株式会社
　　　　　〒162-0804
　　　　　東京都新宿区中里町29番3号
　　　　　菱秀神楽坂ビル9F
　　　　　TEL 03-3513-4511
　　　　　FAX 03-3513-4512
　　　　　www.ibcpub.co.jp

印 刷 所　株式会社シナノパブリッシングプレス

©IBC Publishing 2018

落丁本・乱丁本は小社宛にお送りください。
送料小社負担にてお取り替えいたします。
本書の無断複写（コピー）は
著作権法上での例外を除き禁じられています。

ISBN 978-4-7946-0529-0

Printed in Japan